DECISION MODELS IN
ACADEMIC ADMINISTRATION

edited by
Albert C. Heinlein
Department of Administrative Sciences
Kent State University

published by
Decision Science Institute
Center for Business and Economic Research
Graduate School of Business Administration
KENT STATE UNIVERSITY   KENT, OHIO 44242

DISTRIBUTED BY THE KENT STATE UNIVERSITY PRESS

COLLEGE OF BUSINESS ADMINISTRATION
GRADUATE SCHOOL OF BUSINESS ADMINISTRATION
Gail E. Mullin . . . . Dean
CENTER FOR BUSINESS AND ECONOMIC RESEARCH
Anant R. Negandhi . . . . Director

Library of Congress Cataloging in Publication Data

Decision Sciences in Academic Administration Conference, Kent State
   University, 1973.
   Decision models in academic administration.
   Sponsored by the Decision Science Institute.
   Includes bibliographies.
   1. Decision making in school management — Mathematical models — Con-
gresses. 2. School management and organization — Mathematical models —
Congresses.
I. Heinlein, Albert C., 1924-   ed. II. Ohio. State University, Kent. Decision
Science Institute. III. Title.
LB2806.D37 1973   658'.91'378   74-11585
ISBN 0-87338-167-X

Library of Congress Catalog Card Number 74–11585

ISBN: 0–87338–167–X   ISBN: 0–87338–168–8

Cloth bound $7.50   Paper bound $4.75

PREFACE

This volume provides an unusually complete overview of the need for decision models in academic administration. It covers the work which has been done to date, the nature of on-going research, suggestions for further research, and an inquiry into the problems of implementing academic information and decision models.

The material herein was first presented at the Decision Sciences in Academic Administration Conference, held at Kent State University in May, 1973. The Conference was sponsored by the Decision Science Institute, formed by the decision sciences faculty at Kent State to encourage research which will develop more systematic approaches to administrative decisions. Academic administration was selected as the first year's topic because the current crisis in education has made it an area of great concern.

Participation in the Conference was purposely limited to forty individuals who have demonstrated interest in the area, or who have expressed a desire to become involved in either applying or developing models for academic administration. In addition to the formal presentations, the Conference was devoted to small-group interaction during three workshops which dealt with (1) management information and program planning and budgeting systems; (2) simulation models; and (3) mathematical models. Summaries of the ideas generated in these workshops are also reported in this volume.

Vaughn Huckfeldt's delphi study of "Change in Higher Education Management" provides interesting insights into the kinds of changes anticipated by a panel of academic experts. Roger Schroeder's "A Survey of Operations Analysis in Higher Education" provides useful background on the modeling efforts which have taken place at major research centers, as well as an extensive bibliography. Administrators may also find his second paper, "Four Approaches for the Use of Management Science in University and College Administration," quite useful. Robert Smith and John Anderson provide a summary of the workshop in this area titled "Rational Planning Crisis in Higher Education."

Simulation models for resource allocation in education have been available for several years but are only now beginning to make a real impact. The papers by Les Foreman, and Gary Andrew and Madelyn Alexander discuss three large-scale applications. A workshop summary, "The Effectiveness of Simulation Models in Academic Administration," by Robert Krampf and Albert Heinlein, considers some of the major problems which may be encountered in implementing and using simulation models.

The papers by Robert Wallhaus, Sang Lee and Laurence Moore, and James Dyer present some of the more promising mathematical models. The workshop summary. "The Application of Mathematical Models to Academic

Decision Making," is by J. Randall Brown and James Morris. It considers possible strategies for implementing mathematical models, as well as opportunities for further research.

The editor wishes to express his deep appreciation to each of the speakers, and to the organizations they represent. Likewise, thanks go to the workshop moderators and reporters who performed the monumental task of summarizing and interpreting two days of vigorous and often conflicting discussion, and to all of the participants—each of whom made a substantial contribution to the success of the Conference. Special thanks also go to Dr. Ian MacGregor, vice president for planning at the University of Akron, who provided the assembled theoreticians and practitioners with an administrator's reaction to the decision science approach to university administration.

We would also like to express our appreciation to The Institute of Management Science for permission to reproduce Roger Schroeder's "Survey of Operations Analysis in Higher Education," and to the National Center for Higher Education Management Systems at WICHE for permission to reproduce the papers by Vaughn Huckfeldt and Robert Wallhaus which provided the basis for their discussion of "Analytical Modeling Efforts at NCHEMS."

The Decision Science Institute is also most grateful to Kent State University, and particularly to President Glenn A. Olds; Dr. Gail E. Mullin, Dean of the College of Business Administration; Dr. Anant R. Negandhi, Director of the Center for Business and Economic Research; Dr. Donald Domm, Chairman of the Department of Administrative Sciences; and to Dr. Gerald E. Ridinger, Director of the Bureau of Management Development, for their encouragement and support.

A.C.H.

TABLE OF CONTENTS

Page

*SECTION I: MANAGEMENT INFORMATION AND
DECISION SYSTEMS*

CHANGE IN HIGHER EDUCATION MANAGEMENT   1
Vaughn E. Huckfeldt

**A SURVEY OF MANAGEMENT SCIENCE IN
UNIVERSITY OPERATIONS**   13
Roger G. Schroeder

**FOUR APPROACHES FOR THE USE OF
MANAGEMENT SCIENCE IN UNIVERSITY AND
COLLEGE ADMINISTRATION: A COMPARISON**   29
Roger G. Schroeder

**RATIONAL PLANNING CRISIS IN
HIGHER EDUCATION**   39
Robert D. Smith, John J. Anderson

SECTION II: SIMULATION MODELS

**IMPACT OF THE CAMPUS MODEL ON
DECISION PROCESSES IN THE ONTARIO
COMMUNITY COLLEGES**   47
Les Foreman

**THE MINNESOTA AND COLORADO
EXPERIENCES WITH THE CAMPUS
PLANNING SYSTEMS**   65
Gary M. Andrew, Madelyn D. Alexander

**A FEDERAL PLANNING MODEL FOR ANALYSIS
OF ACCESSIBILITY TO HIGHER EDUCATION:
AN OVERVIEW**   69
Vaughn E. Huckfeldt

**THE EFFECTIVENESS OF SIMULATION MODELS
IN ACADEMIC ADMINISTRATION**   91
Robert F. Krampf, Albert C. Heinlein

SECTION III: MATHEMATICAL MODELS

**A RESOURCE ALLOCATION AND PLANNING
MODEL FOR HIGHER EDUCATION**　　　　　97
Robert A. Wallhaus

**ACADEMIC RESOURCE ALLOCATION MODELS
AT U.C.L.A.**　　　　　109
James S. Dyer

**GOAL PROGRAMMING FOR ADMINISTRATIVE
DECISIONS IN HIGHER EDUCATION**　　　　　121
Sang M. Lee, Laurence J. Moore

**THE APPLICATION OF MATHEMATICAL
MODELS TO ACADEMIC DECISION MAKING**　　　　　131
James G. Morris, J. Randall Brown

CHANGE IN HIGHER EDUCATION MANAGEMENT*+

Vaughn E. Huckfeldt
National Center for Higher Education in Management Systems
Western Interstate Commission for Higher Education

The identification of change in postsecondary education is today more important than ever before for reasons expressed by Clark Kerr (1971) in an address presented at the Twenty-Sixth National Conference on Higher Education:

> Higher Education in the United States is facing a period of uncertainty, confusion, conflicts, and potential change, and it has little to guide it in its past experience. For most of its three and one-third century history, it has had a manifest destiny and through the period from 1920–1970 was marked by rapid change and some student unrest. Two factors remained constant: public belief in and support of higher education, and the campus and society were both changing, but in compatible ways. This is no longer so and higher education is faced with a staggering number of uncertainties: (1) the direction of change that will be taking place in a society that is ever more divisive, and in a world that is undergoing a cultural revolution; (2) the impact of the new educational technology; (3) its proper functions in terms of teaching, research, and services; (4) the governance of the institutions; and (5) financing.[1]

NCHEMS recognized this need to gain insights into the changes that would be likely to occur in postsecondary education during the next five to fifteen years, and during early 1972 a survey was undertaken that focused on the long range directions of postsecondary education. The major purpose of this survey was to assure that the management concepts, tools, and procedures that NCHEMS is currently developing or has planned will be relevant when they are ready for implementation.

The survey method used was the DELPHI method, including computer technology and multiple rounds of questionnaires, which is a far cry from the

---

*This study is part of a research program supported by the Ford Foundation, Grant Number 700–0434. Ideas and opinions expressed in this paper are those of the author and do not necessarily reflect an official position of NCHEMS, WICHE, or the Ford Foundation.

+This paper was originally published in 1972 by the National Center for Higher Education Management Systems at Western Interstate Commission for Higher Education. The editor wishes to express appreciation to the NCHEMS for its permission to reproduce this material.

[1] Clark Kerr, "Destiny—Not so Manifest." Address presented at the Twenty-Sixth National Conference on Higher Education, American Association for Higher Education, Washington, D.C., 1971.

original DELPHI technique—the Delphic oracles of Greece in the sixth century B.C. Then, the priestess Pythia merely sat on her golden tripod in the great temple of Apollo and, after reaching a trance-like state, she spoke the oracles, answering all questions in a frenzied babble.

The DELPHI technique, as NCHEMS has used it, was developed by futurologists Dr. Olaf Helmer and Norman Dalkey at the RAND Corporation as a technique for soliciting and combining the opinions of experts. Its primary initial uses were in the area of technological forecasting, but more recently it has been employed to identify agreement concerning organizational goals and objectives. The key characteristics of the DELPHI approach are:

1. The anonymity of the survey panel members.

2. A statistical analysis of the panel's responses.

3. The use of controlled feedback to panel members in a series of successive rounds.

Basically, the DELPHI method attempts to bring together a group of experts in a "conference call" or "seminar" setting. But, through anonymity of the panel, the DELPHI method prevents the influence of some members of the panel from overriding or unduly swaying the opinions of the other panel members. In some sense, it prevents an important or very articulate expert from controlling the panel's opinion. The DELPHI method summarizes the responses to one round of questions and provides this information to the survey panel with the next round of questions. In this way, the experts, while remaining anonymous, still communicate with each other in a limited fashion.

The NCHEMS DELPHI posed six questions over five survey rounds:

Round   I: What are the possible changes that might take place?

Round II: What will be the impact of a change, if it occurs, and what is the likelihood of the change occurring?

Round III: Posed these same questions again, this time with feedback of the Round II results.

Round IV: Asked the same questions as in Rounds II and III and posed the additional question: In what time period will the change occur?

Round V: Repeated the question introduced in Round IV with feedback, and added two questions: Should this change occur, and who will most affect this change?

In evaluating the results of the NCHEMS survey, one must consider who the panel members were as well as their answers. The names of the panel members cannot be given, as they remain anonymous in order to retain the confidentiality in which the panel gave their responses. Table 1 shows the primary position held by the 385 individuals who participated in the survey, as well as the number holding that position and the percentage responding during the survey.

Before examining the results of the survey it is important to consider that the analysis is subject to certain qualifications:

1. The make-up of the survey panel is open to all sorts of questions, but any panel would have exhibited one sort of bias or another.

2. The survey was completed before the final passage of the Higher Education Act of 1972.

3. Undoubtedly, the panel members had different interpretations of when a change can be said to have occurred widely enough to have an impact on planning and management.

A more detailed description of the survey methodology, qualifications, and a discussion of the criteria used in analyzing the survey data can be found in the complete analysis report of the survey, *A Forecast of Changes in Postsecondary Education.*

Table 1
PANEL RESPONSE ACCORDING TO PRIMARY POSITION

Primary Position	Number in Group	Percent Responding
Federal Congressmen	4	25
State Governors or Executive Administrators	4	100
State Legislators	9	56
Federal Staff Members for (HEW, USOE, U.S. Congress)	13	92
Staff of Statewide Coordinating or Governing Board	39	97
Foundation Staff Members	5	100
Lay Board Members, Trustees, or Regents	7	100
Members of a National Education Association	15	93
Board Members or Commissioners of an Education Board or Commission	13	92
Staff Members for an Education Board or Commission	19	100
Members of an Accreditation Agency	4	75
Consultants in Postsecondary Education	11	90
Students	15	93
Members of an Educational Bargaining Unit	3	100
Faculty	12	100
College or University MIS Director or Staff	39	100
Department Chairmen or Deans of Academic Instruction	15	93
College or University Finance Administrators or Staff	30	97
College or University Directors or Staff for Institutional Research	51	98
College or University Directors of Staff for: Admissions, Personnel, Physical Plant, etc.	19	100
College or University Presidents or Vice-Presidents	54	93
Members of the Education Press	4	50
	385	94%

THE RESULTS OF THE NCHEMS SURVEY

The 118 statements about change that were utilized in the survey covered six broad areas of postsecondary education:

1. Access and Participation

2. Competence and Performance

3. Educational Structure and Components (with major subcategories: Program Content, Administration, Faculty, and Students)

4. Resource Availability

5. Planning and Management

6. Nontraditional Education

The purpose of this section, then, is to present for each of these areas a set of general interpretations that have resulted from the author's analysis of the panel responses. It should be emphasized that these are the author's interpretations of the opinions of 385 persons affected by and involved in postsecondary education today. In arriving at these interpretations, particular reference has been made to the section "What Are the Changes" of the complete analysis report.

In each of the areas, the forecast provided by the NCHEMS DELPHI is as follows:

Access and Participation

Perhaps the most important area of agreement among the survey panel was that by the late 1970's postsecondary education will be more readily accessible to all. Students will tend to be more casual about their participation in the postsecondary education process. They will attend full-time when they think it suits their needs and part-time on other occasions. They will increasingly drop in and out of the educational process as they desire, but there is no evidence that high school students will delay entrance into postsecondary education. The federal government will be a principal force encouraging this increased accessibility.

With increased accessibility, in what areas of postsecondary education will students participate?

At the graduate level, an increasing percentage of students will seek professional degrees as opposed to Ph.D. degrees. At the undergraduate level, there will be no discernible shift in emphasis from bachelor's degrees to associate degrees, but the proportion of students in vocational programs will increase, and the manpower needs of society will receive increased attention.

Competence and Performance

While certification on the basis of competency will eventually become more routine, major changes are not likely to occur until after 1980, if at all. In the 1970s, little success will be met in modifying the rigid structure of certification and evaluation. However, it should be noted that student experience in the nonacademic community will be increasingly accepted for academic credit. The analysis also shows that the emphasis on grades will not decrease.

Structure of the Educational System

Postsecondary education will be more coordinated, the ease of transferability of credit will increase, and institutions will gradually begin to share resources. But the panel felt these changes would not be likely to cause institutions to become more alike. The control that may influence changes in the postsecondary education structure will arise without the federal government increasing its emphasis on developing a master plan for postsecondary education; it will come more from state level agencies.

Program Content

The content of programs in postsecondary education will shift to give social problems and public service increased emphasis by the late 1970s. However, this will not include ethnic studies, which will probably undergo a relative decrease in emphasis during this period. While institutions will place more emphasis on social problems, the role of institutions as direct change agents in society will not increase substantially.

Emphasis on research as a major program of institutions will tend to stabilize, but postsecondary education itself will be the topic of more of the research and development activities. In four-year colleges and universities there·will be an increased emphasis on upper-division and graduate programs.

Faculty

The relationship of the faculty to management will be a subject of ferment during the 1970s. There will be an increase in collective bargaining. Understandably, then, the panel felt that faculty will not have a larger role in the formal governance of their institution. It is unlikely that faculty tenure will be eliminated, but the faculty will have less freedom relative to workload and activities. There will be an increased emphasis on teaching and little change in the "publish or perish" concept.

Students

Housing for students will generally be reduced. However, cutbacks in other student services, such as recreation, health, and counseling, will not be likely to occur until the late 1970s, if at all. Institutions will be likely to drop the "in loco parentis" concept. Institutions will not provide a larger governance role for students prior to the end of the decade.

Educational Technology

Changes in educational technology will occur later than other changes in the educational structure. Even after 1980, the emphasis on the techniques of teaching and processes of learning will not have changed relative to the emphasis on subject matter. Changes that seem likely to occur include increased flexibility and versatility in educational facilities and increased use of TV, computers, and new instructional technologies. The increased flexibility will extend to the facilities themselves, which will be used more hours of the day and more days of the year. The most distant prediction of the panel finds psychopharmacy and psychoelectronics unlikely to come into use to induce or augment learning before the 1990s, if at all, and the majority felt such a change should not occur.

Resource Availability

Funding sources will give closer scrutiny to the utilization of available resources, and new planning and management techniques will be used in this scrutiny. At the same time, the panel felt it unlikely that the general level of resources available to postsecondary education will decline. Smaller and smaller amounts will be spent for new capital construction in larger institutions.

In spite of the labels that may be attached, funding from federal sources will increasingly deemphasize general aid. Total federal and state dollars to private institutions and to students directly will increase during the next decade.

Planning and Management

Educational outcomes will be an integral part of the analysis of postsecondary education by the late 1970s. The use of new planning and management techniques will increase, as will the requirement for comparability and compatibility of data. The faculty and students involved in the governance of institutions will continue to support their individual group directions rather than the collective goals and objectives of the institution.

Nontraditional Education

The panel felt that the roles of nontraditional institutions *vis-a-vis* those of colleges and universities would not change in the 1970s. This perceived stability is probably explained by the make-up of the panel, which was heavily oriented toward traditional higher education. It also no doubt reflects the fact that the survey was conducted prior to the passage of the new higher education legislation.

In What Areas Will Change Occur?

Let us consider the relationship of the total panel's opinions about the areas in which changes will most likely occur, the areas in which change will have the greatest impact, and the areas in which change will occur first. Table 2 shows that changes in planning and management are the most likely to occur and that the educational structure is least likely to change.

In considering the impact of changes, the panel felt changes in planning and management would have the highest impact and changes in the educational structure the least impact. The only difference between the impact and likelihood columns is in the items "access and participation" (seen as more likely to increase and yet lesser in impact), and "resource availability" (seen as a high-impact factor not likely to increase). The panel's responses forecast changes in access and participation occurring earliest

Table 2
TOTAL PANEL OPINION BY GROUPS OF CHANGE STATEMENTS

HIGH IMPACT	HIGH LIKELIHOOD	EARLY TIME
PLANNING AND MANAGEMENT	PLANNING AND MANAGEMENT	ACCESS AND PARTICIPATION
RESOURCE AVAILABILITY	ACCESS AND PARTICIPATION	RESOURCE AVAILABILITY
COMPETENCE AND PERFORMANCE	COMPETENCE AND PERFORMANCE	PLANNING AND MANAGEMENT
NONTRADITIONAL EDUCATION	NONTRADITIONAL EDUCATION	EDUCATIONAL STRUCTURES
ACCESS AND PARTICIPATION	RESOURCE AVAILABILITY	NONTRADITIONAL EDUCATION
EDUCATIONAL STRUCTURES	EDUCATIONAL STRUCTURES	COMPETENCE AND PERFORMANCE
LOW IMPACT	LOW LIKELIHOOD	LATER TIME

and changes in competence and performance occurring last. One possible reason that changes in competence and performance will occur later than other changes is that this is the only area in which the panel consistently identified one force (the faculty) as most hindering change.

Finally, an interesting note about which subgroups of the panel feel changes in general are more likely to occur with a greater impact and at an earlier time. When the panel subgroups are ranked on the basis of a combined high impact, high likelihood, and earliest time score, as shown in Table 3, the order of the panel subgroups is from federal down through the organizational levels to the students, with the federal members saying more can be done at an earlier time and with a greater impact.

Table 3
THE OPINION OF PANEL SUBGROUPS RANKED BY
HIGH IMPACT, HIGH LIKELIHOOD, AND EARLIEST TIME

Highest Impact and Likelihood, Earliest Time	Federal
	National Education Associations
	Regional Organizations
	State
	Department Chairman and Faculty
Lowest Impact and Likelihood, Latest Time	Students

THE IMPLICATIONS FOR CHANGE IN MANAGEMENT

An analysis of the forecasted changes based on the survey results highlights some of the following important impacts on planning and management.

The forecast that postsecondary education will be more accessible to all leaves one with the question, "Just what is this increased assessibility?" The answer to this question may influence changes in management at the institutional, state, and national levels. As part of the process by which the federal government determines the financing plan for higher education, Congress will consider the impact of alternative financing plans on accessibility. Accessibility can mean access to admissions, access to continued success in higher education, or access to a degree or certification. The funds required for increased accessibility are much greater if it means removing the roadblocks to a higher degree rather than initial access or admission. The management process of the institution could also change in considering effective methods of dealing with potential dropouts and adjusting the system to ensure their access to a degree.

Institutional managers will need to find a way to cope with the admissions problems of increased numbers of in-and-out students—

stopouts. One of the problems that will arise as more and more students drop in and out of the education process is the likelihood of a decline in stability of enrollments and a corresponding increase in the complexity of forecasts used to project enrollments. This means it will be more difficult to identify future needs for institutional capacity. A second problem will be to keep a complete history of students who have dropped out and their current educational status.

As the number of part-time students increases, administrators will be hard pressed to provide the necessary services, which in many cases require the same amount of administrative resources for processing full- or part-time students, and it will be much more difficult for higher education to deal with students as individuals.

Changes in the management of certification will be required to control the granting of external degrees and to prevent the establishment of "diploma mills." On the other side, accreditation associations will need management flexibility to deal with an increased variety of higher education institutions offering a wider choice of programs, including vocational programs.

As credit toward certification is provided for work in areas other than formal academic programs, institutional management will need to develop methods to define the amount of credit to be given for work or service experience.

The changes in faculty and their relationship to the institution will require institutional management to live in a collective bargaining environment. The administrator may use information from faculty activity analyses to assist in the bargaining process, but the main problem the administrator will face is the decrease in resource flexibility as faculty-institution relations become more rigid. The solutions open to management may include revising hiring policies for the institution (i.e., joint appointments, part-time faculty, etc.), and making definite choices between faculty and new technology.

As public service gains increased importance and the research and instruction functions do not decline, management will have more difficulty in allocating funds to programs. The cost of new technological equipment for instruction will eventually present additional funding difficulties. This, coupled with a more rigid instructional structure (i.e., resource scrutiny, faculty relations, etc.), means the flexibility of dollars will decrease. One area in which there may be a shift in funds is from certain student support activities, particularly housing, to other needy areas.

As state agencies become a major force in governance changes in education, institutional management will need to learn to live with this force as well as with an increased amount of federal interaction. The new management tools will give some basis for maintaining institutional control by providing the information necessary to communicate to and with federal, state, and faculty forces. There will also be an increasing need to develop and implement standard procedures for reporting and exchanging information. The use of such new planning and management procedures will require additional time of administrators and managers for understanding the new techniques and the information they can provide.

Management will, in many cases, be faced with the governance of an internal struggle between the forces supporting change and those opposing change. As the administration is forced to take sides in resolving such conflicts, the freedom of managerial movement relative to these opposing forces will be restricted.

A DESCRIPTION OF OTHER SURVEY REPORTS

This report deals with the major highlights of the forecasted changes and their impact on management. Additional information can be obtained from the following NCHEMS reports:

1. *A Forecast of Changes in Postsecondary Education*, the complete analysis and forecast of changes in postsecondary education made in the NCHEMS DELPHI survey.

2. *Methods for Large-Scale DELPHI Studies*, a documentation of the methodology used by NCHEMS in conducting a DELPHI study with a large panel. This report should benefit future NCHEMS studies and the educational community, since the large number of factors impinging on postsecondary education will dictate panels of more than 100, and large-scale DELPHI studies do present a number of technical and logistical problems.

3. *Documentation of Large-Scale DELPHI System Software*, a complete documentation of the computer software developed for the NCHEMS DELPHI survey. This software is available as Type II NCHEMS software, available at cost but with no guarantee or program support.

4. *Data from the NCHEMS Future Planning and Management Systems Survey*, a complete documentation of the NCHEMS DELPHI survey data base. This data base is available at cost to anyone wanting to do additional research on the data.

REFERENCES

Alexander, Madelyn D.
 1973 *The Implementation of CAMPUS/COLORADO at the University of Colorado*, University of Colorado, Boulder, Colorado, to be presented at the AIR 1973 Annual Conference, Vancouver, British Columbia, Canada, to be published.
Alexander, Madelyn D.
 1973 *The Implementation of CAMPUS/COLORADO: Boulder, Colorado Springs, Denver, Progress Report No. 1*, University of Colorado, Boulder, Colorado.
Andrew, Gary M.
 1973 *CAMPUS at Colorado*, University of Colorado, Boulder, Colorado, presented at SCUP 1973 Spring Conference "Let's End the Confusion about Cost-Simulation Models." Washington, D.C., to be published.
Andrew, Gary M.
 1973 Academic Planning—*Using a Cost Simulation Model for Structuring Information and Communication*, University of Colorado, Boulder, Colorado. (Draft)

Andrew, Gary M.; David C. Cordes; Alden C. Lorents.
  1971   Project PRIME Report No. 14, Mid-Year Report.
Andrew, Gary M.
  1971   Project PRIME Report No. 16, *Final Report: Project PRIME*, Minnesota
          Higher Education Coordinating Commission.
Cordes, David C.
  1970   Project PRIME Report No. 2, *An Introduction to Project PRIME and
          CAMPUS MINNESOTA.*
Cordes, David C.
  1971   *Resource Analysis Modelling in Higher Education: A Synthesis*,
          Ph.D. Dissertation, School of Business Administration, University of
          Minnesota.
Lorents, Alden C.
  1971   *Faculty Activity Analysis and Planning Models in Higher Education*,
          Ph.D. Dissertation, School of Business Administration, University of
          Minnesota.
Mason, Thomas R.
  1973   *The Purpose of Analytical Models: The Perspective of Model User*, University
          of Colorado, presented at SCUP 1973 Spring Conference "Let's End the
          Confusion about Cost Simulation Models." Washington, D.C., to be
          published.

A SURVEY OF MANAGEMENT SCIENCE IN UNIVERSITY OPERATIONS*+

Roger G. Schroeder
University of Minnesota

INTRODUCTION

This paper surveys the development and use of management science in universities and colleges. For purposes of exposition, the survey is organized into four areas: 1) Planning, Programming, and Budgeting Systems; 2) Management Information Systems; 3) Resource Allocation Models; and 4) Mathematical Models. Together, these areas include the primary uses of quantitative methods for decision making in institutions of higher education. We limit the scope to institutional studies only. We do not include work in the statewide, regional, or national education areas, although a significant amount of work has been done there too.

The paper covers each of the four areas in some detail. However, it does not attempt to list every reference. Rather, this survey points out significant references and it provides an interpretation and unification of the material. Ample bibliographies and citations are given so that additional work can be easily found, if desired.

The major sources of material used were *Research in Education* (RIE),[1] *Current Index to Journals in Education* (CIJE), *Management Science*, *Operations Research*, and *IFORS Abstracts*. It may be noted that a large part (about 70 percent) of the work referenced in this paper comes from unpublished reports rather than published articles. This is due to the rapidly expanding nature of research in the field and the lag between results and journal publication.

---

* In the preparation of this paper, valuable comments were obtained from Stanley Johnson of the University of Minnesota; David C. Cordes of Managment Decision Systems, Inc., St. Paul, Minnesota; and George B. Weathersby of the University of California. An earlier version of this paper was presented to the 41st National Meeting of the Operations Research Society of America, April 26–28, 1972.

+ This article originally appeared in *Management Science*, Vol. 19, No. 8 (April, 1973). The editor wishes to express appreciation to the publishers of *Management Science* for their permission to reprint this material.

[1] RIE is published monthly by Educational Resources Information Center (ERIC), Office of Education, Washington, D.C. For those doing work in the field of education, it is essential to become familiar with RIE, which contains abstracts of all unpublished reports collected by the ERIC Clearing Houses, and the companion volume CIJE, which abstracts published articles from 530 journals in the field of education.

There have been three other surveys of work in the field of higher education. One of the earliest was conducted by Rath (1968:B373–384). He traced the development of the field in several areas and indicated that a large part of the work prior to 1968 was on computerized class scheduling. Two recent surveys, limited exclusively to modeling in higher education, are Weathersby (1972), and Systems Research Group (1972). In addition to these surveys, two useful bibliographies are: Case and Clark (1967:22) and Hufner (1968:25–101). The most comprehensive bibliography is the one by Hufner, which is recommended for work published prior to 1968. Finally, a useful reference is the *Proceedings of the First Symposium on Operations Analysis of Education* held in 1967.[2]

From a historical perspective, it is interesting to note several early papers calling for the application of systems analysis and quantitative methods to education. Early papers were written by Kershaw and McKean (1959), Platt (1962:408–418), and Schroeder and Rath (1965). Although these papers and others called for applications of quantitative techniques, little was accomplished until about 1965 when applications and research began to rapidly expand.

PLANNING, PROGRAMMING, AND BUDGETING SYSTEM

A Planning, Programming, and Budgeting System (PPBS) has often been defined in terms of its name. Planning refers to setting of organizational objectives and goals; programming refers to identifying and evaluating programs or alternatives which meet those objectives; and budgeting refers to providing the resources to support the programs. But PPBS is more than just a new method of budgeting; it includes planning and analysis functions as well. The analysis part of PPBS is usually accomplished by the cost-effectiveness approach, which considers the costs and benefits of alternative programs. Such analysis is an integral part of a PPB system.

One of the essentials of PPBS is an output oriented budget which is organized along the lines of the outputs of the organization. This type of budget allows comparisons and identification of competing programs on an effectiveness basis. In higher education, commonly used output categories are Instruction, Research, and Public Service. There seems to be wide acceptance of these categories among different institutions, thus providing a basis for common program structures, at least at the aggregate level.

Two extensive bibliographies on PPBS in education have recently been completed (Nelson, 1970; Cordes, 1971). Each of these bibliographies contains about 1000 citations. This indicates the tremendous literature on the subject written mainly within the last five years. Due to the volume of work, our short survey can only cover the major trends and the most significant work. For other bibliographies see Piele and Bunting (1969), Hagan (1968), and McGivney and Nelson (1969). Cordes (1971), Van Wijk, *et el.* (1969),

---

[2] *Socio-Economic Planning Science*, Pergamon Press, Volume 2, Numbers 2/3/4, April 1969, pp. 103–520.

Weathersby and Balderston (1971), and Hitch (1968:37–47) also are excellent surveys and studies of PPBS in higher education.

The greatest emphasis which is being placed on PPBS in higher education at the present time comes from the National Center for Higher Education Management Systems (NCHEMS) at WICHE.[3] They have developed, with the encouragement of the U.S. Office of Education, a standard Program Classification Structure (PCS) (Gulko, 1971). This structure is being developed so that institutions can have comparable data on costs of programs and to facilitate statewide, regional, and national planning. The commonality will, of course, provide a tremendous potential for comparisons of programs and coordinated planning.

There have been no successful ongoing applications of a comprehensive PPBS. Probably the most widely known partial implementations are at the University of California and Ohio State University. In addition, there are numerous other universities which have some form of a PPBS or are in the process of developing one. References which discuss implementations are Cordes (1971), Van Wijk, et al. (1969), and Balderston and Weathersby (1972). The extent to which PPBS will be implemented depends heavily on how well it can be integrated into the universities' daily operating and financial control systems. If the PPB system remains separate from the operating system, plans will not necessarily mesh with operating decisions and the result will be an ineffective system.

To achieve an effective PPB system, it is necessary to measure outputs or benifits of educational programs. But output measurement in education is one of the most difficult problems. Although some work has been done, no really satisfactory progress has been made. References on the general problem of establishing and measuring educational objectives are Balderston (1970), Keller (1970), Huff (1971), and Lawrence, Weathersby, and Patterson (1970). Furthermore, a large amount of data is summarized on forty-seven different goals in universities by Gross and Grambsch (1968). We cannot expect real progress in the evaluation of educational programs until better tools of measurement are available.

MANAGEMENT INFORMATION SYSTEMS (MIS)

A Management Information System (MIS) generally refers to collection, storage, and retrieval of information for both planning and control functions. The information in an MIS will usually include financial and budgeting information, as well as other information, such as student records, enrollment data, course demand data, facility planning data, and so on. The scope of an MIS may be quite broad or limited, depending on the particular application. However, even limited MIS's are usually computerized to handle the large amount of data involved. A survey of MIS in education is by Piele (1970).

Management Information Systems for education are still in the design phase, with only a few implementations to date. Three universities which

---

[3] WICHE is the Western Interstate Commission on Higher Education at Boulder, Colorado.

have implemented various forms of an MIS are reported by Kornfield (1969). These universities are the following: University of Utah, Ohio State University, and the University of Illinois. Kornfield includes in his discussion of these systems the organization, historical development, design, implementation, costs, and benefits.

Perhaps the best perspective of recent efforts is given by Minter and Lawrence (1969:113) in the proceedings of a symposium on "Management Information Systems: Their Development and Use in Administration of Higher Education."[4] This report contains several excellent papers on a wide range of MIS issues and topics. It also contains a very good bibliography of about 500 references and it indicates forty-five institutions which are pursuing MIS programs.

There are currently two major projects in the design and testing of MIS's for higher education: the NCHEMS Program and the Stanford Project INFO. The NCHEMS work is closely related to their PPBS effort in standard program classification structures and data elements. The work on project INFO (Information Network for Operations) is reported by Gwynn (1969). This project is developing a set of procedures to facilitate the construction and maintenance of a data base. It also includes extensive software development, programming, and file structure design efforts.

One of the issues in MIS design is the question of how to design a data base. Advocates of the comprehensive approach argue that we should include a large amount of data in the data base since we cannot hope to predict the data which management will need. This type of approach is advocated by project INFO. The other approach argues that decision making should be analyzed and analytic models constructed where possible to determine what data should be included in the data base. Administrators should then be supplied with analysis and information from this system. The NCHEMS approach is along these lines.

RESOURCE ALLOCATION MODELS

Resource allocation models[5] relate the inputs of the educational process to the resources required. They translate enrollment projections into demand for courses, faculty, facilities, and support activities. The required resources are then costed and aggregated for various output reports. The purpose of these models is to simulate the effects of changes in enrollment or in the "technology" (student-teacher ratios, class size, etc.) on the resources required. Two excellent surveys on resource allocation models are by Weathersby and Weinstein (1970) and Casasco (1970).

CAMPUS
There have been several different resource allocation models developed to date. The first model to be introduced was CAMPUS (Computerized

---

[4] Symposium held in Washington, D.C., April 24–26, 1969, sponsored by WICHE and the U.S. Office of Education.

[5] Another commonly used descriptive term for these models is "cost simulation models."

Analytical Methods in Planning University Systems) at the University of Toronto, Ontario, Canada (Judy and Levine, 1965). From enrollment inputs, CAMPUS develops activity workloads and the associated faculty, space, and equipment required. Usually an activity is taken to be an individual course, although it may be defined at a higher level. From given enrollments, students are allocated among curriculums (e.g., first semester MBA) according to a specified distribution vector. This provides a given number of students in each curriculum. Activity loads are then computed from specified probabilities that a student in a given curriculum will engage in a particular activity. These activity loads are aggregated across all curriculums and appropriate activities are grouped by cost centers (usually academic departments) and by programs. After applying resource factors to the activity loads, the result is the resouce requirements of the given input enrollments over future periods (Judy, 1969A, 1969B, 1969C).

There are several versions of CAMPUS available. CAMPUS I, II, III, and IV were all pilot models or special application versions developed at Toronto. CAMPUS V is available to the public at nominal costs and is a hardware simulator only, with no input/output routines provided. CAMPUS VI is a time sharing version which allows access from several institutions. And the latest version, CAMPUS VII, is a scaled-down version of CAMPUS VI. However, full implementation of any of these versions requires extensive data and programming support.

The CAMPUS models have been applied at a number of locations: the University of Toronto, the Toronto University Medical School, the twenty Colleges of Applied Arts and Technology in Ontario, Wheaton College, Hostos College, Duke Univeristy Health Sciences, and four colleges in Minnesota. Details on the Minnesota experience are contained in Cordes (1971), and the other applications are reported by Mowbray and Levine (1971). Even though CAMPUS has been tested at several institutions, only limited usage to date has been achieved as part of an ongoing management program.

RRPM

Another well known resource allocation model is the RRPM (Resource Requirements Prediction Model).[6] An excellent description of this model is contained in Gulko (1971:37). RRPM documentation is available in Gulko and Hussain (1971), Hussain (1971), and Hussain and Martin (1971). RRPM has recently been completed and has been tested by eight pilot institutions. The major difference between CAMPUS and RRPM is that RRPM is more aggregated, and it does not have as much flexibility in data input format. The lowest level of aggregation in RRPM is the discipline level, e.g., engineering, agriculture, business. It is not designed to simulate to the level of individual courses.

In general, the RRPM model proceeds from enrollment projections to course demands to faculty requirements to faculty costs and related support

---

[6] The RRPM model is a revised version of the Cost Simulation Model (CSM) originally developed by Weathersby (1967).

costs. For each time period and each degree major, student enrollment is an input by grade level (1, 2, 3, 4, graduate MS, Ph.D., and Special). A second input is a set of matrices of student demands for each type of course or the so called Induced Course Load Matrix (ICLM). These matrices, one for each major, indicate the average credit hours that a student at a particular grade level will demand at each course level in each of the instructional disciplines. From these matrices and the enrollment inputs, the RRPM model accumulates the required credit hours over all majors. The result is the student demand for instruction in each discipline and course level. Faculty requirements are then generated by applying average faculty teaching load levels. These requirements are finally costed by applying unit cost factors.

There have been two interesting papers which analyzed the RRPM model. The first paper by Jewett, *et al.* (1970), was a study of the stability and accuracy of the projections obtained from the ICLM. In this report seven quarters of data on the ICLM were obtained from Humboldt State College in California. Based on these data, a projection was made of student credit hours demanded in each discipline and course level. These projections varied by as much as 40 percent from the actual demands. The projections were then aggregated in accordance with the RRPM model to predict faculty requirements by discipline. In these aggregated projections, the error dropped to nine per cent of actual faculty levels. The question remains open as to whether this order of accuracy will be typical in other institutions and whether it is too low or not.

The other paper which analyzed RRPM was written by Hopkins (1971:467–478). The purpose of his paper is best described by Hopkins as: "(1) to give a simple description of a university cost simulation model; and (2) to raise some questions about its expense, accuracy, and usefulness as a tool for university management." Hopkins concludes that, "these models are suitable mainly for making cost-per-student calculations under current operating conditions and that it is questionable whether the expense of building in a large amount of detail for this purpose can be justified." He suggests as an alternative a very aggregated model developed by Oliver, Hopkins, and Armacost (1970). This model provides an explicit choice of decision variables at the highest policy level of university planning and requires only minimal data. Although Hopkins' views are very controversial, they provide a beginning dialogue on the usefulness of resouce allocation models.

OTHER RESOURCE ALLOCATION MODELS

There are two other operational resource models. The consulting firm of Peat, Marwick, Mitchell, and Co. has a timesharing model called SEARCH. This model is similar to RRPM in level of aggregation and the handling of student demands for courses (Keane and Daniel, 1970; Scarborough and Daniel, 1968). The SEARCH model and its earlier versions have been tested and implemented at several small colleges. The Midwest Research Institute has also developed a model called HELP/PLANTRAN which is operational but much smaller than those already mentioned

(McKelvey, 1970). Finally, there are three other resource allocation models which have been used exclusively for research purposes to date: (1) Koening, et al. (1969), developed a resource model at Michigan State University; (2) Thompson (1970) reports on the University of Washington model; and (3) a model has been developed at Tulane University by Firmin, et al. (1967).

MATHEMATICAL MODELS

This section deals with mathematical formulations, optimization problems, and mathematical models in higher education. The work which has been done is divided into three categories: (1) student planning, (2) faculty staffing, and (3) optimal resource allocation. Only some of the major studies in each area are outlined here in order to provide a perspective and a starting point for those interested in further work.

Student Planning

References in the student planning category include scheduling students to classes, enrollment projections, and student flows through an institution. The earliest work done in this area is the scheduling of students by computer (Oakford, Allen, and Chatterton, 1967; Tomei, 1969). Nevertheless, in 1969 a survey report[7] indicated that only partial implementation was in effect. The survey was conducted of ninety-six colleges and universities, including seventy with ten thousand or more students. Of this group, only one-third indicated that they used computers to schedule students into classes. This indicates the lag between research reports and actual implementation which is true of much of the management science work in education. Recent articles dealing with the scheduling of students to classes have been written by Shoeman and Bhaumik (1970), Shapley, et al. (1966), Smith (1971), and Swart (1972). Prediction of enrollments, student flows, and graduation rates have been areas of considerable recent activity. This work will be classified into two groups: Markov type models and all other approaches. An excellent survey of student flow models is by Lovell (1971).

The largest amount of work on student flow problems has been done with Markov models or variations of the basic Markov formulation. In these formulations a state is usually the student's grade (freshman, sophomore, etc.), and perhaps his major. The number of students in each state then depends in a Markovian fashion on the numbers in previous states, the transition rates, and the new admissions. Models of this type were first studied by Gani (1963:400–409), and Young and Almond (1961:246–250). They have been refined and developed by Harden and Tcheng (1971:467–473), Johnson (1972), Marshall, Oliver, and Suslow (1970), and Oliver (1968). In addition, most of the resource allocations models (CAMPUS, MSU, SEARCH) have Markov student flow sections which predict future enrollments of students. An input student flow driver is also under development for RRPM (Johnson, 1972).

---

[7]"Report on Registration Procedures at Ninety-Six Colleges and Universities," Cincinnati University, Dept. of Instructional Studies, February 1969.

An alternative approach to the prediction of student flow is the cohort method, which relies on longitudinal data collected from histories of cohorts over time. This approach is formulated as a network model by Oliver and Hopkins[8] (1971A, 1971B).

The advantage of this method over Markov models is that it can represent processes which do not have the simple Markov property. But the cohort models require substantially more data.

Another method of projecting student flows is the work load method. Marshall and Oliver (1970:193–206) used this approach to develop a "constant work load model" of student attendance and enrollment. It is based on the notion that a constant amount of work is required for a degree, and it predicts enrollments based on the work required and the estimated probabilities of attending, vacationing, dropping out, and graduating, given attendance in each period. Another work load model has been developed by Balachandran and Gerwin (1972) for prediciting individual course enrollments. In their study, "work" is defined as completion of prerequisite courses.

Turksen (1970) developed a model to forecast enrollments for individual courses which recognizes student preferences, curriculums, and uncertainties. This too, of course, is a departure from Markov models. Finally, Jewett (1970) has done some work on admissions policy. He developed a model which evaluates tradeoffs between tuition, student aid, and admissions decisions.

Faculty Staffing

In the faculty area there have also been several studies of flows. Oliver (1968B) investigated nontenured and tenured faculty movements and the effect on new appointments and promotion policies by constructing an equilibrium model of the process. Goody, Hopkins, and Oliver (1969) also developed a faculty flow model to predict faculty retirement rates. Rowe, Wagner, and Weathersby (1970) developed a control theory solution to a staffing problem. They investigated the effect of hiring policies on the optimal control of faculty rank distributions. Bartholomew (1969) also studied a control theory formulation of faculty appointments and promotions. A Markov faculty flow model was applied to the engineering faculty at the University of California, with results reported by Branchflower (1969).

Finally, Breneman (1969) reported on an empirical study of faculty input coefficients in a linear workload model. These are the coefficients which relate enrollment levels to faculty levels required. He found (1) relatively high instability in most coefficients; and (2) aggregated figures are not necessarily more stable than less aggregated projections.

Optimization of Resource Allocation

There have been a few recent attempts at development of optimal resource allocation models. One approach is the use of optimal control

---

[8] In addition to student flows, these models include faculty levels and instruction costs.

theory ideas developed by Weathersby and others at the University of California. The model includes decision variables of undergraduate admissions, faculty hiring and new facilities over an n-period planning horizon. A differential dynamic programming approach is used to find decision variables which maximize the "value" achieved (see Weathersby, 1970, and Wagner and Weathersby, 1971). Another approach is due to Geoffrion, *et al.* (1971). They use a multicriterion optimization model to assist in departmental resource allocation decisions. The model is structured to provide value tradeoffs for department chairmen within institutional and resource constraints.

Wallhaus (1971) has developed an interesting goal programming model of optimal resource allocation. It determines the number of students to be admitted to each grade level and program which achieves desired degree goals as closely as possible within resource constraints. However, at present, a model of even a small college is too large to solve. Another goal programming model was proposed by Lee and Clayton (1972). Their model is much smaller and considers a variety of goals for resource allocation within a college.

Turksen and Holzman (1970) reported work on a departmental resource allocation model. It allows choices among teaching, research, and other activities via linear and quadratic objective functions. Fox, *et al.* (1967), also reported on an allocation model of faculty between research and teaching. A linear programming model with interaction between department heads and a dean is proposed. Finally, Andrew (1971) designed an assignment model to assign professors to courses. It maximizes a weighted combination of faculty preference and teaching effectiveness while meeting all restrictions. An extensive survey of "Mathematical Programming Models in Educational Planning" is given by McNamara (1971).

Research Programs on Administration in Higher Education
There are three large programs of research on administration in higher education. These programs are (1) the Ford Foundation Program for Research in University Administration at the University of California, Berkeley, in the Office of the Vice President-Planning; (2) the NCHEMS Program (National Center for Higher Education Management Systems) in Boulder, Colorado; and (3) the program at the Institute for the Quantitative Analysis of Social and Economic Policy, University of Toronto, Ontario, Canada, with the offshoot private group called the Systems Research Group (SRG).

The Ford program at Berkeley has been closely associated with mathematical modeling. The specific areas include objectives and measurement of output, decision models, flow models, and organizational questions. The status of the program and publications is listed in "A Program of Research in University Administration," October 1972.[9]

The program at NCHEMS centers primarily around RRPM, program classification structures, student flows, faculty activity analysis, outputs of

---

[9] Available from Ford Project, 2288 Fulton Street, Berkeley, California 94720.

higher education, and state and federal planning systems. This is a large and intensive program of research, development, training, and implementation. The latest report of activities and publications is contained in "NCHEMS Director's Annual Report."[10]

The program at the University of Toronto and SRG has dealt with resource allocation questions and university systems in general. Their most well known work was the development of the CAMPUS model.

The organization for Economic Cooperation and Development (OECD) has been active in the applications of Management Sciences to education. They have held three conferences entitled, "Mathematical Models in Educational Planning" (1967), "Budgeting Program Analysis and Cost-Effectiveness in Educational Planning" (1968), and "Efficiency in Resource Utilization in Education" (1969). The Proceedings contain many excellent articles.

FUTURE DIRECTIONS

In reviewing the literature, there appear to be four areas in need of further research.

1. Investigation is needed of the suitability of Markov models in predicting student flows, faculty flows, or course demands. Studies in this area are needed to determine the best levels of aggregation, the stability of the projections, and preferred methods of choosing past data to produce sufficient accuracy for planners' needs. Although a variety of Markov models have been proposed, only two studies, by Jewett, *et al.* (1970), and Breneman (1969), have been done on the suitability of the methods.

2. A detailed investigation is needed of what university administrators do and the information which is required for their decisions. At the present time there is not sufficient data available in this regard. The data would be useful for (1) subjectively assessing the worth of the present models and information systems and (2) designing better MIS's. The only investigation known along these lines is the one on secondary education reported by Rittenhouse and Chorness (1969).

3. More work needs to be done on the measurement of the outputs of higher education. Presently, this area is very weak. More studies would also be useful in relating inputs to the outputs of the education process. Although progress is being made in the areas of PPBS, future results will be limited without better methods for measuring outputs and relating outputs and inputs to specific programs.

4. Although many models and techniques have been developed, there seems to be a lack of actual implementation. This is probably due to inadequate integration of the models into the operating system of the institution. Unless the outputs of models are understood by administrators, they will not be used. To improve success in implementation, the systems approach should be used to study the decision process, related information problems, and the organization to determine how models and techniques

---

[10] Available from WICHE, P.O. Drawer P, Boulder, Colorado 80302.

might be used. Some work in this direction is reported by Adams and Schroeder (1972).

REFERENCES

Adams, Carl and Roger Schroeder.
1972   "Design of College Analysis and Management Systems," Working Paper, Graduate School of Business, University of Minnesota.
Andrew, Gary M. and Robert Collins.
1971   "Matching Faculty to Courses," *College and University*, Vol. 46.
Balachandran, K. R. and Donald Gerwin.
1972   "Variable Work Models for Predicting Course Enrollments," School of Business Administration, University of Wisconsin, Milwaukee.
Balderston, F. E.
1970   "Thinking About the Output of Higher Education," Ford Research Program in University Administration, University of California, Berkeley.
—— and George B. Weathersby.
1972   "PPBS in Higher Education Planning and Management: Part II, The University of California Experience," Ford Research Program in University Administration, University of California, Berkeley.
Bartholomew, D. J.
1969   "A Mathematical Analysis of Structural Control in a Graded Manpower System," Report P-4, Ford Research Program in University Administration, University of California, Berkeley.
Branchflower, N. H., Jr.
1969   "A Case Study of the Distribution of Faculty Within the College of Engineering at the University of California, Berkeley, 1960–68," Ford Research Program in University Administration, University of California, Berkeley.
Breneman, David.
1969   "The Stability of Faculty Input Coefficients in Linear Workload Models of the University of California," Paper 69–4, Ford Research Program in University Administration, University of California, Berkeley.
Casasco, Juan A.
1970   "Planning Techniques for University Management," Report for the American Council on Education with the ERIC Clearinghouse on Higher Education, Catholic University, p. 77.
Case, C. Marston and Stephen Clark.
1967   "A Bibliographic Guide to Operations Analysis of Education," National Center for Educational Statistics (DHEW), Washington, D.C., Division of Data Analysis and Dissemination, p. 22.
Cordes, David.
1971   "Resource Analysis Modeling in Higher Education: A Synthesis," Ph.D. Dissertation, University of Minnesota.
————.
1970   "Planning, Programming and Budgeting Systems in Education: Concept, Operations Status and a School of Business Administration Example," Management Information Systems Research Center, University of Minnesota, p. 61.
Firmin, Peter A., S. S. Goodman, T. G. Hendricks and J. J. Linn.
1967   "University Cost Structure and Behavior," Tulane University.
Fox, K. A. *et al.*
1967   "Formulation of Management Science Models for Selected Problems of College Administration," Iowa State University.
Gani, J.
1963   "Formulae for Projecting Enrollments and Degrees Awarded in Universities," *Journal of the Royal Statistical Society*, A126, pp. 400–409.

Geoffrion, A. M., J. S. Dyer, and A. Feinberg.
 1971　"Academic Departmental Management: An Application of an Interactive Multi-Criterion Optimization Approach," Report P-25, Ford Research Program in University Administration, University of California, Berkeley.
Goody, Robert, David Hopkins, and R. M. Oliver.
 1969　"Faculty Retirement Systems," Ford Research Program in University Administration, University of California.
Gross, Edward and Paul Grambsch.
 1968　"University Goals and Academic Power," American Council on Education.
Gulko, Warren W.
 1971　"The Resource Requirements Prediction Model 1 (RRPM-1): An Overview," TR-16, NCHEMS, p. 37.
─────.
 1971　"Program Classification Structure," Preliminary Edition (Revised), NCHEMS.
── and K. M. Hussain.
 1971　"A Resource Requirements Prediction Model (RRPM-1): An Introduction to the Model," TR-19, NCHEMS.
Gwynn, John.
 1969　"The Data Base Approach to a Management Information System," Minter, John and Ben Lawrence (eds.), *Management Information Systems: Their Development and Use in Administration of Higher Education*, proceedings of a seminar held in Washington, D.C., (available from ERIC Reproduction Service, ED042427), p. 114.
Hagen, John.
 1968　"Program Budgeting," UCLA Center for Study of Evaluation, Report No. CSER7, UCLA, Los Angeles, California.
Harden, Warren R. and M. T. Tcheng.
 1971　"Projection of Enrollment Distributions with Enrollments' Ceilings by Markov Processes," *Socio-Economics Planning Sciences*, Vol. 5 pp. 467–473.
Hitch. Charles J.
 1968　"The Systems Approach to Decision-Making in the Department of Defense and the University of California," *Operational Research Quarterly* (U.K.), Vol. 19, Special Conference Issue, pp. 37–47.
Hopkins, David S. P.
 1971　"On tne Use of Large-Scale Simulation Models for University Planning," *Review of Educational Research*. Vol. 41, No. 5, pp. 467–478.
Huff, Robert A.
 1971　"Inventory of Educational Outcomes and Activities," Technical Report No. 15, NCHEMS.
Hufner, Klaus.
 1968　"Economics of Higher Education and Educational Planning—A Bibliography," *Socio-Economic Planning Sciences*, Vol. 2, pp. 25–101.
Hussain, K. M.
 1971　"A Resource Requirements Prediction Model (RRPM-1): Guide for the Project Manager," TR-20, NCHEMS.
── and J. N. Martin.
 1971　"A Resource Requirements Prediction Model (RRPM-1): Report on the Pilot Studies," TR-21, NCHEMS,
Jewett, Frank I., *et al.*
 1970　"The Feasibility of Analytic Models for Academic Planning: A Preliminary Analysis of Seven Quarters of Observations on the Induced Course Load Matrix," California State Colleges, p. 133.
Jewett, J. E.
 1970　"College Admissions Planning: Use of a Student Segmentation Model," Report P-23, Ford Research Program in University Administration, University of California, Berkeley.

Johnson, Richard F.
1972   "NCHEMS Student Flow Model SFM-IA: An Introduction" (preliminary draft), NCHEMS.
Judy, Richard W.
1969A   "System Analysis and University Planning," *Socio-Economic Planning Sciences*, Vol. 2, NOS 2/3/4.

──────.
1969B   "Systems Analysis for Efficient Resource Allocation in Higher Education," Minter and Lawrence (eds.), *Management Information Systems: Their Development and Use in Higher Education*, WICHE.

──────.
1969C   "Simulation and Rational Resource Allocation in Universities," *Efficiency in Resource Utilization in Education*, Paris: OECD, pp. 255–285.
────── and J. Levine.
1965   "A New Tool for Educational Administrators," Report to the Commission on the Financing of Higher Education, Toronto; University of Toronto Press.
Keane, G. F. and J. N. Daniel.
1970   "Systems for Exploring Alternative Resource Commitments in Higher Education (SEARCH)," Peat, Marwick, and Mitchell.
Keller, John E.
1970   "Higher Education Objectives: Measures of Performance and Effectiveness," Paper P-7, Ford Research Program in University Administration, University of California, Berkeley.
Kershaw, J. A. and R. N. McKean.
1959   "Systems Analysis and Education," Rand Corporation RM-2473-FF, Santa Monica, California.
Koenig, Herman and M. B. Keeney.
1969   "A Prototype Planning and Resource Allocation Program for Higher Education," *Socio-Economic Planning Science*, Vol. 2, Nos. 2/3/4.
Kornfield, Leo L.
1969   "Advanced Applied Management Information Systems in Higher Education: Three Case Studies," Minter and Lawrence (eds.), *Management Information Systems: Their Development and Use in Administration of Higher Education*, ERIC Reproduction Services, ED042427.
Lawrence, Ben, George Weathersby, and Virginia Patterson.
1970   "The Outputs of Higher Education," NCHEMS.
Lee, S. M. and E. R. Clayton.
1972   "A Goal Programming Model for Academic Resource Allocation," *Management Science*, Vol. 18, No. 8.
Lovell, C. C.
1971   "Student Flows Models, A Review and Conceptualization," TR-25, NCHEMS.
Marshall, K. T. and R. M. Oliver.
1970   "A Constant Work Model for Student Attendance and Enrollment," *Operations Research*, Vol. 18, No. 2, pp. 193–206.
────── and S. S. Suslow.
1970   "Undergraduate Enrollments and Attendance Patterns," Administrative Studies in Higher Education Report No. 4, Chancellor's Office and Operations Research Center, University of California, Berkeley.
McGivney, J. H. and William C. Nelson.
1969   "PPBS for Education, Vol. III: An Annotated Bibliography," Final Report, Ohio State University.
McKelvey, J.
1970   "HELP/PLANTRAN: A Computer Assisted Planning System for Higher Education," Midwest Research Institute.
McNamara, James F.
1971   "Mathematical Programming Models in Educational Planning," Review of

Educational Research, Vol. 41, No. 5.

Minter, John and Ben Lawrence (eds.)
1969   *Management Information Systems: Their Development and Use in the Administration of Higher Education.* Available from ERIC Reproduction Service, EDO42427, p. 113.

Mowbray, George and Jack Levine.
1971   The Development and Implementation of CAMPUS: A Computer-Based Planning and Budgeting System for Universities and Colleges," *Educational Technology.*

Nelson, William C.
1970   "PPBS for Educators, Vol. IV: A Research Bibliography Final Report," Ohio State University, Report Bibl-4.

Oakford, R. V., D. W. Allen, and L. A. Chatterton.
1967   "School Scheduling Practice and Theory," *Journal of Educational Data Processing,* pp. 16–50.

Oliver, R. M.
1968A   "Models for Predicting Gross Enrollments at the University of California," Report No. 68–3, Ford Research Program in University Administration, University of California, Berkeley.

――――.
1968B   "An Equilibrium Model of Faculty Appointments, Promotions, and Quota Restrictions," Report No. 69–10, Ford Research Program in University Administration, University of California, Berkeley.

―――― and David S. P. Hopkins.
1971A   "Instructional Costs of University Outputs," Operations Research Center, University of California, Berkeley.

――――.
1971B   "An Equilibrium Flow Model of a University Campus." Operations Research Center, University of California, Berkeley.

――――, ―――― and Robert Armacost.
1970   "An Academic Productivity and Planning Model," Report No. 3, Ford Research Program in University Administration, University of California, Berkeley.

――――, ――――, and ――――.
1969   Organization for Economic Co-operation and Development, Education
1968   and Development Technical Reports, *Efficiency in Resource Utilization*
1967   *in Education; Budgeting Programme Analysis and Cost-Effectiveness in Educational Planning; Mathematical Models in Educational Planning.*

Piele, Philip.
1970   "Management Information Systems: Analysis of Literature and Selected Bibliography," ERIC Clearinghouse on Educational Administration, University of Oregon, EDO43113.

―――― and David Bunting.
1969   "Program Budgeting and the School Administration: A Review of Dissertations and Annotated Bibliography," Review Series No. 2, Oregon University, DHEW Contract BR-80353.

Platt, William J.
1962   "Education-Rich Problems and Poor Markets," *Management Science,* Vol. 8, No. 4, pp. 408–418.

Rath, G. I.
1968   "Management Science in University Operation," Management Science, Vol. 14, No. 6, pp. B-373–384.

Rittenhouse, Carl H. and M. H. Chorness.
1969   "A Survey of the Decision Processes and Related Informational Requirements for Educational Planning and Innovation," presented at Western Psychological Association Convention, ERIC No. EDO41357.

Rowe, S., W. G. Wagner, and G. B. Weathersby.
1970   "A Control Theory Solution to Optimal Faculty Staffing," Ford Research
        Program in University Administration, University of California, Berkeley.
Scarborough, Collin W. and J. N. Daniel.
1968   "Management Use of Simulation in Long-Range Planning for Colleges and
        Universities," paper presented at TIMS/ORSA meeting, p. 23.
Schoeman, Milton and Bora Bhaumik.
1970   "A Class Scheduling Model and Algorithm," University of Texas.
Schroeder, Roger G. and Gustave I. Rath.
1965   "The Role of Mathematical Models in Educational Research," *Psychology
        in the Schools*.
Shapley, L. S., D. R. Fulkerson, A. Horelick, and D. M. Weiter.
1966   "A Transportation Program for Filling Idle Classrooms in Los Angeles,"
        Rand Corporation, P-3405, Santa Monica, California.
Smith, R. L.
1971   "Accommodating Student Demand for Courses by Varying Classroom
        Size Mix," *Operations Research*, Vol. 19, No. 4.
Swart, William W.
1972   "A Course Scheduling Problem: Model Development, Analysis and Solution
        Algorithm," West Virginia University (presented to 41st national meeting
        of ORSA).
Systems Research Group (SRG).
1972   "The State of the Art in Educational Cost Modeling Systems," SRG,
        Toronto.
Thompson, R. D.
1970   "Higher Education Administration: An Operating System Study Utilizing a
        Dynamic Simulation Model," in *Corporate Simulation Models*, ed. Schrieber,
        University of Washington.
Tomei, Mario J.
1969   "An Analysis of the Experience and Effects of Computer Assisted Scheduling
        in Selected Institutions of Higher Education," Temple University, Philadel-
        phia, Pennsylvania.
Turksen, I. B. ang A. C. Holzman.
1970   "Micro Level Resource Allocation Models for Universities," 37th ORSA
        Conference, Washington.
_____.
1970   "A Micro Level Forecasting Model of Student Enrollment," 37th ORSA
        Conference, Washington.
Van Wijk, P. Alfons, R. W. Judy, and J. B. Levine.
1969   "The Planning, Programming, Budgeting System in Universities: A Study of
        Its Applicapility and Some Preliminary Designs," Document No. 24, The
        Institute of Policy Analysis, University of Toronto, p. 54.
Wagner, G. W., and George B. Weathersby.
1971   "Optimality in College Planning, A Control Theoretic Approach," Ford
        Research Program in University Administration, University of California,
        Berkeley.
Wallhaus, Robert A.
1971   "A Resource Allocation and Planning Model in Higher Education,"
        NCHEMS.
Weathersby, George.
1967   "The Development and Applications of a University Cost Simulation
        Model," Graduate School of Business Administration and Office of
        Analytical Studies, University of California, Berkeley, p. 125.
_____.
1970   "Educational Planning and Decision Making: The Use of Decision and
        Control Analysis," Paper P-6, Ford Research Program in University
        Administration, University of California, Berkeley.

—— and M. C. Weinstein.
1970   "A Structural Comparison of Analytical Models for University Planning,"
        Ford Research Program in University Administration, University of California,
        Berkeley.

————— .
1972   "Tools and Techniques for Planning and Resource Allocation in Higher
        Education," Ford Research Program in University Administration, University
        of California, Berkeley.
—— and F. E. Balderston.
1971   "PPBS in Higher Education Planning and Management: Part I, An
        Overview," Ford Research Program in University Administration, University
        of California, Berkeley.
Young, A. and G. Almond.
1961   "Predicting Distributions of Staff," *Computing Journal 3*, No. 4, pp.
        246–250.

FOUR APPROACHES FOR THE USE OF MANAGEMENT SCIENCE IN UNIVERSITY AND COLLEGE ADMINISTRATION: A COMPARISON

Roger G. Schroeder
University of Minnesota

INTRODUCTION

Management Science has been applied to problems in university and college administration during the past ten years. (See Schroeder, 1972, and Weathersby, 1972, for extensive reviews of the literature.) Over this period, the following four approaches have been evolved:

1. Resource Planning Models

2. PPBS

3. Individual Analytic Studies

4. Management System Analysis.

This paper compares and discusses the above four approaches. It attempts to provide a better perspective of the four methods for improving university and college administration through Management Science. It should lead to a better understanding of not only the approaches themselves, but their relationship to each other. Each of the four approaches is summarized in turn. We do not present a detailed discussion of any particular model or approach. The major thrust is to highlight the approaches and relate them to each other.

The paper also points out several problems and difficulties that have been experienced in implementing the first three approaches. These difficulties may be characterized by too much attention to models and too narrow a view of the management process. The paper indicates how the fourth approach, Management System Analysis, can overcome these difficulties and lead to improved implementation success.

RESOURCE PLANNING MODELS

Resource planning is a fundamental activity of administrators at all levels in universities and colleges. There is wide agreement that resource planning in general is an absolutely essential part of administration. However, there are many different kinds of resource planning. This leads to different models for different types of planning. No one model can encompass the

29

entire range of resource planning problems. The "value" of a particular model or approach has to be related to the needs of each institution and the types of questions that the model can answer. A model that is extremely useful in one institution may only have limited value in other institutions with different problems. Such differences in value assessments and needs are evident from the pilot studies of the RRPM model (Hussain and Martin, 1971).

Due to the diverse nature of resource planning models, a classification scheme is needed for purposes of comparison. The following scheme is proposed.

1.   Allocation or Prediction Models

2.   Model Inputs and Outputs

3.   Model Technology

These classification characteristics are discussed next.

Resource allocation deals with allocating fixed amounts of resources among various activities. For example, a resource allocation model might accept a college payroll budget as input and determine how it should be allocated between types of faculty, teaching assistants, and staff. In a resource allocation model, the amounts of resources available are inputs and activity levels are outputs of the model. The reverse is true for resource prediction models. They take given activity levels as inputs and the resources required are outputs of the model. For example, a resource prediction model might accept faculty, teaching assistants, and staff levels as inputs and it would determine the resulting budget required.

Resource allocation models are best suited to institutions that are faced with relatively fixed budgets. These institutions must adjust faculty workloads and programs to fit within the budgets available. In the RRPM pilot studies (Hussain and Martin, 1971), Stanford and UCLA indicated this view of their institutions. On the other hand, resource prediction models are best suited to institutions where resources are strongly related to enrollments. In this case, changes in enrollment levels and mix can be expected to directly affect future resource requirements.

Another characteristic of a resource planning model is its inputs and outputs. Inputs and outputs are determined by such considerations as the level of aggregation and the types of resources to be used. A resource planning model is further affected by the choice of technology which establishes the relationship between inputs and outputs. For example, the relationship between faculty workloads and enrollments would be a matter of model technology.

As an example of differences in model types, RRPM (Hussain, 1971) can be compared to CAMPUS (Van Wijk and Russell, 1972); they are both resource prediction models. However, the inputs and outputs are different and so is the model technology. CAMPUS VIII can simulate to the class level and it accepts data on the classes that various majors take. RRPM only simulates to the discipline level and does not accept individual class demand data. In addition, RRPM uses average class sizes, while CAMPUS can use maximum section sizes. Since the models are different, so are the types of questions that can be answered. For example, CAMPUS VIII can be used to simulate changes in individual courses for curriculum planning; RRPM cannot go to that detailed level.

Proforma budget projection models, such as the HELP/PLANTRAN (McKelvey, 1970) model, also deal with resource prediction. Unlike CAMPUS/RRPM, these models do not accept enrollment inputs. They project the budget ahead several years to account for inflation, wage increases, and other gross changes. They are designed to answer a different set of questions than the RRPM/CAMPUS models. Proforma budget models deal with a fairly high level of aggregation and they cannot reflect the changes in resources required due to changes in enrollment mix or size.

Finally, there are a few models that deal with resource allocation, such as Lee and Clayton (1972), Geoffrion, *et al.* (1972), and Schroeder (1972). These models all accept resources as inputs and allocate them to various activities, but they differ in the type of resources considered, level of aggregation, and model technology. They also are designed to answer different types of resource planning questions.

In sum, different resource planning models are designed for different issues. We should not expect one model to be ideally suited for every institution. However, even more fundamental is the question of whether an institution, at a particular point in time, needs resource planning models at all.

It appears that some institutions should spend more effort on clarifying and defining their resource planning process instead of building models. For models to be actually used in resource planning there must be some decision making process. For example, if the planning process forces review of alternatives, then models can be used to help evaluate alternatives. Currently, many colleges and universities do not review alternatives nor do they plan far enough into the future to require the use of planning models. It is not only necessary to make the outputs of models available, the decision process must be oriented to resource planning in the first place.

PLANNING PROGRAMMING AND BUDGETING SYSTEMS (PPBS)

Unlike the resource planning models, the use of PPBS has focused directly on reform of the decision making process. Nevertheless, PPBS has experienced great difficulty in implementation. Weathersby and Balderston (1971), in their excellent review of PPBS, reported: "To our knowledge, a total comprehensive implementation of PPBS has not been achieved in any college or university in the United States." Van Wijk (1969) also reached a similar conclusion in his review of PPBS.

It is difficult to attack PPBS on a conceptual basis. The ideas of output orientation, multi-year planning, program analysis, cost benefit studies, and so on are widely accepted. Nevertheless, PPBS has experienced implementation problems, not only in education but in the Federal government as well.

One of the possible weaknesses of PPBS has been an excessive focus on the program budget document itself. This leads to over-concern with defining programs and arranging costs in program format at the expense of any real program analysis. If there is no analysis of program costs and benefits, decision making cannot be improved. It might be better to gather data on the costs and benefits of specific programs, as needed, than to insist on obtaining all of this data in the form of a program budget.

In order to be effective, a PPB System must identify and measure outputs. Of course, this is true of any other planning system as well. NCHEMS is pursuing a vigorous program aimed at improving output measurement. Nevertheless, this remains as one of the critical problems, not only in PPBS but in educational planning as a whole.

Some institutions have been trying to improve their internal planning process in the spirit of PPBS without using the program budget. These universities include Princeton (1972), Minnesota (1971), Illinois at Champaign-Urbana (1972), and MIT (1970). Although each planning system is different, they all are aimed at improving goal definition, program review, and analysis. Unfortunately, such individual developments do not lend themselves to the exchange of uniform information for Federal and statewide planning purposes. This is a fundamental issue that has not been widely recognized: the conflict between an institution's needs for planning data and the requirements of various government units.

We can perhaps avoid the difficulties that have been experienced with PPBS by searching for. broad principles that can be used in the design of planning systems. Each institution could apply these principles in a way that suits its own individual needs; nothing so constraining as a program budget need be required. Broad planning principles must address the following areas:

1. Institution-wide goal definition

2. Goal measurement criteria

3. Methods of translating goals into policy and programs

4. A means of acquiring resources and allocating them to programs

5. Methods for evaluating programs and policy

Many institutions do not have a systematic planning process of the type suggested above. In this era of tight financial constraints, institutions must develop this type of process to insure vitality and progress in meeting their aims and objectives.

INDIVIDUAL ANALYTIC STUDIES

The third approach that has been used to introduce Management Science into institutional management is the use of individual analytic studies. These studies often include a mathematical model and they are aimed at specific decision problems. Examples of this approach are given on the next page.

1. Development of the Minnesota Cost Development Model is discussed by Johnson (1972). This effort involved the construction of a historical cost allocation model. It was used to determine the unit costs of a degree winner, the cost per year for each major, and a cost per student credit hour for each department.

2. A projection of tenured faculty with existing policies was made by Oliver (1968). His analysis indicated that equilibrium could not be reached with the existing tenure promotion rates at Berkeley.

3. Hopkins (1972) conducted a study of the effect of an early retirement plan at Stanford. He found that early retirements could be offered at about the same cost by inducing highly paid full professors to retire early and replacing them with assistant professors at a lower salary level.

These are only a few examples of analytic studies aimed at specific decision problems. A large number of additional studies are referenced in the preceeding article.

The analytic study approach offers three principle features:

1. Studies can be focused on areas where there is a high potential payoff. One can select problems that are badly in need of analysis.

2. If models are used, they can be tailor-made to fit the particular problem under study. The model can be developed to fit the problem and not *vice versa*.

3. The studies can be small in nature, requiring limited resources and limited organizational reform.

Because of the small study focus of the approach, it is more evolutionary in nature than PPBS or resource planning models. Progress can be made in small steps without changing the entire system.

Of course, there are also potential difficulties with the analytic study approach.

1. These studies require a relatively high degree of management planning and control to insure that the analysis produces practical outputs. Analysts can become enamored with the technical aspects of model building to the exclusion of user impact and results.

2. This approach requires a high degree of technical competence. It is extremely difficult to build models that are realistic and useful. Since the models are tailor-made, each application requires a major technical effort.

A more complete discussion of how this approach can be used is presented by Schroeder and Adams (1972).

The analytic study approach has much merit. It is essentially the same approach that has been used to implement Management Science in business firms for twenty-five years. But even this approach tends to focus almost exclusively on problem solution rather than problem definition. The next approach advocates problem definition and a wider system focus.

MANAGEMENT SYSTEM APPROACH*

The fourth approach considers the management system of an institution as a whole. It aims to improve the decision making process by studying the existing institutional process before making changes. It does not assume that any specific type of model or technique will be used in advance. The focus of this approach is on the process of management, the way that decisions are made, and the information used.

The Management System approach consists of three separate phases.

1. *Review:* In this phase the existing management system is documented. This documentation includes a description of what decisions are made, who makes them, how often they are made, what information is used, and so on. Data is collected both by interviews with administrators and by analysis of written reports. The data provides a description of how the current system operates and where potential weaknesses exist.

2. *Design:* The design of an improved management system is based on the review phase. It involves a definition of objectives and goals, specific activities that have to be undertaken, information to support decision making, and a management control system to insure progress is being made toward goals. No specific models or techniques are envisioned in advance for this phase, but specific models would be included where appropriate.

3. *Implementation:* This phase involves the development of specific methods to carry out design changes. It includes training and education in new procedures and evaluation of progress at all points. This is perhaps the most difficult phase and a significant amount of time is required for its completion.

There is currently a research effort at the University of Minnesota to develop and test the Management System approach. The first phase, review, is being tested at ten colleges in the Midwest during the summer of 1973. A detailed description of the data collection methods and instruments is presented by Schroeder and Adams (1973). The complete three-phase approach is being tested at Augsburg College over a two-year period. Augsburg is serving as the initial test college for the entire approach.

The so called Management System approach is different from the other approaches that have been used in several major respects.

---

*The approach discussed in this section has been developed jointly by Carl Adams and the author at the University of Minnesota.

1. The approach focuses on problem definition instead of only problem solution. The whole review phase is aimed at trying to systematically document the institution's problems. It is not until the design phase that problem solution comes into play. At that time the focus is on designing a process so that an institution can solve its own problems, rather than providing solutions for them.

2. The approach takes time to complete. About one year is needed for review and design and a second year for implementation. Because of the wide range of problems that are reviewed, it is not desirable to do a "quick" analysis.

3. The approach is being designed for small colleges. Although a similar approach could be developed for major universities, that is not part of the initial plan.

4. The approach not only addresses planning issues, it considers management control, information, organization, and operations. Some of the other approaches have been too narrow in that they have not properly integrated planning with the other aspects of management.

5. No mathematical models are required for the success of the approach. The approach can achieve significant results through improvement of the management process alone.

6. Any models or techniques that are included in the new system would be tailor-made for the institution concerned. The approach does not advocate one general model that can be applied to all institutions.

The Management Systems approach provides a more comprehensive view of university management problems than has been taken in the past. This wider view is not only a strength but a potential source of weakness. The approach must maintain a broad focus, but at the same time provide specific results. We believe this is possible, if the approach is properly used.

CONCLUSIONS

The use of Management Science in university and college administration is at a critical point in its development. Although many models and techniques have been developed, their impact on the decision making process has been minimal in some institutions. To achieve better results, a systems-wide view and more emphasis on the decision process is needed.

Decision process improvement is needed at all levels of educational administration. Such improvement involves, in some cases, definition of new decision procedures and in other cases improvement of existing procedures. A specific type of process improvement, such as PPBS, may not be the best approach. Improved decision processes should be designed for each institution based on their own needs, organization, and circumstances. A three-phased management system approach for designing such improved decision processes has been outlined.

Individual analytic studies and models can be effectively implemented in universities and colleges if the efforts are properly organized, planned, staffed, and controlled. Project management is needed to insure that technical aspects of the problem are not over emphasized to the exclusion of results. Sometimes the technical part of these studies is excellent but there is little impact on the decision process.

Improvement in decision making would also benefit from more attention on problem definition rather than problem solution. There has ·been a tendency to focus on solving a particular type of problem where techniques are available, rather than continued emphasis on identifying and formulating problems. This can lead to a good solution for the wrong problem.

REFERENCES

Geoffrion, A. M., J. S. Dyer and A. Feinberg.
1972   "An Interactive Approach for Multi-Criterion Optimization, with an Application to the Operation of an Academic Department," *Management Science,* Vol. 19, No. 4 (December, Part I).

Hopkins, David S. P.
1972   "Analysis of a Faculty Early Retirement Program," Academic Planning Office, Stanford University.

Hussain, K. M.
1971   "A Resource Requirements Prediction Model (RRPM-1): Guide for the Project Manager," TR-20, NCHEMS.

Hussain, K. M., and J. S. Martin (eds.)
1971   "A Resource Requirements Prediction Model (RRPM-1): Report on the Pilot Studies," TR-21, NCHEMS, October.

Johnson, Stanley C.
1972   "The Analytical Studies Experience at the University of Minnesota," Graduate School Research Center, Minneapolis, Minnesota, April 26.

Lawrence, Ben, George Weathersby, and Virginia Patterson (eds.)
1970   "Outputs of Higher Education: Their Identification, Measurement, and Evaluation," NCHEMS, July.

Lee, S. M. and E. R. Clayton.
1972   "A Goal Programming Model for Academic Resource Allocation," *Management Science,* Vol. 18, No. 8, April.

Massachusettes Institute of Technology.
1970   "Growth, Equilibrium, and Self-Renewal," Report of the Commission on MIT Education.

McKelvey, J.
1970   "HELP/PLANTRAN A Computer Assisted Planning System for Higher Education," Midwest Research Institute.

Oliver, R. M.
1968   "An Equilibrium Model of Faculty Appointments, Promotions, and Quota Restrictions," Report No. 69–10, Ford Research Program in University Administration, University of California, Berkeley.

Princeton University, The Treasurer.
1972   "Budgeting and Resource Allocation at Princeton University," Report of a Ford Foundation Project, June.

Schroeder, Roger G.
1973   "A Survey of Management Science in University Operations, *Management Science,* Vol. 19, No. 8, April.

Schroeder, Roger G.
1972   "Resource Planning in University Management by Goal Programming,"
        Graduate School of Business Administration, University of Minnesota,
        Working Paper No. 6, September.
Schroeder, Roger G., and Carl R. Adams.
1973   "The Review of Management Systems: An Approach for Educational
        Institutions," Working Paper, Graduate School of Business Administration,
        University of Minnesota, April.
Schroeder, Roger G., and Carl R. Adams.
1972   "The Effective Use of Management Science in University Administration,"
        Working Paper No. 9, Graduate School of Business Administration,
        University of Minnesota, Minneapolis, Minnesota, December.
University of Illinois at Urbana-Champaign, Office of the Vice Chancellor for Academic
Affairs.
1972   "Preliminary Report of the Study Committee on Program Evaluation
        (SCOPE)," April 7.
University of Minnesota, Office of the Vice President, Academic Administration.
1971   "Accountability and Educational Criteria: University Planning for Selective
        Growth," A joint report of the University Committees on Educational
        Policy and Resources and Planning, July.
Van Wijk, A. P. and R. S. Russell.
1972   "State of the Art in Educational Cost Modeling," Systems Research Group,
        Toronto, Canada, November 8.
Van Wijk, A. P., R. W. Judy, and J. B. Levine.
1969   "The Planning, Programming, Budgeting System in Universities: A Study
        of Its Applicability and Some Preliminary Designs," Document No. 24,
        The Institute of Policy Analysis, University of Tornto, October.
Weathersby, George.
1972   "Tools and Techniques for Planning and Resource Allocation in Higher
        Education," Ford Research Program in University Administration, University
        of California, Berkeley, January.
Weathersby, George, and F. E. Balderston.
1971   "PPBS in Higher Education Planning and Management: Part I, An Over-
        view," Ford Research Program in University Administration, University of
        California, Berkeley, December.

RATIONAL PLANNING CRISIS IN HIGHER EDUCATION

Robert D. Smith and John J. Anderson
Kent State University

INTRODUCTION

This section represents an attempt to integrate the collective wisdom of approximately thirty experts in the fields of program budgeting and management informations systems who participated in a workshop session held during the 1973 Decision Science Conference at Kent State University. Credit for innovative concepts, empirical experiences, and practical advice contained in this paper belongs to workshop participants. The authors accept full responsibility for misinterpretations, omissions, or other errors in reporting.

THE NEED FOR PLANNING

Between 1950 and 1970 planning emphasis in higher education was upon growth. Faculty consensus on decisions was not necessary, primarily because no one was getting hurt. Existing programs did not undergo evaluation. When a new program was desired, there was money available to initiate it. Today, planning and decision making require reallocation of funds and occasionally even the elimination of certain programs. Consequently, the planning process has become much more burdensome, complex, and important.

It appears that the future will force even more hard decisions upon educational administrators. It seems inevitable that programs will have to be abolished, and perhaps even some institutions will be dissolved or drastically reorganized. Indeed, there exists a rational planning crisis in higher education. Which tools or models can be used to resolve this crisis remains uncertain.

At the University of Minnesota, a task force developed a document titled *Toward 1985*, which provided an overall strategy for the university. One of the points stressed in this document is that the University of Minnesota is not going to attempt to be "all things to all people—that those programs which are to be stressed and funded are those which make the University of Minnesota unique."

Strategy at the Massachusetts Institute of Technology has been to lead the nation in very new fields. But as enrollment decreases, the ten years of theory building generally required to establish new disciplines implies that some established programs will have to be cut to support basic research. It has also been pointed out that it is better to cut five per cent of an organization's programs than to strangle everyone by across-the-board five per cent budget cuts. Some sort of Growth Committee has been recommended to pick new areas for funding.

One workshop participant suggested that "education, as a profession, has been incompetent, incompetent because it waited to plan until it was forced to do something that it should have been doing all along." Education is on the defensive now because it never bothered to take the offensive, to justify with hard data what was being accomplished. Consequently, by default, legislators are now making decisions which they have no business making. As an example, a large university recently instituted a new law school. The legislators visited the campus and told the administration they should use the old library for the law school. They *told* them rather than *asking* the university whether they had sufficient space. They actually dictated where the law school would be located.

At another school, faculty salary represents seventy-five per cent of total costs and eighty per cent of the faculty are expected to be there for the next thirty years. In addition, empty dormitories, built to house a currently nonexistent student body, are located throughout the campus. How much sophistication in planning was needed to foresee the end of growing enrollment? In view of these and many other examples, is there any doubt that universities are in dire need of formalized short and long range planning?

FORMAL PLANNING TECHNIQUES

Program budgeting, or PPBS, as it is sometimes referred to, has been defined in a number of different ways. During the workshop session the following definition was offered: program budgeting is an organizational change model; a rational, systematic planning approach with emphasis on goals, program coordination, and measures of effectiveness; a movement away from line item budgeting.

Much of the glamour which accompanied program budgeting in the Federal Government during the middle 1960's has become tarnished. Few secondary education institutions are presently using this technique, and it is doubtful whether decisions in institutions of higher education are being changed by it at this point. It is apparent, however, that declining enrollments, faculty and student unionization, and increased pressures for accountability will cause some form of program budgeting to become more important in higher education in the immediate future.

During the workshop it was concluded that only certain organizations are currently ready for a rational planning approach, such as program budgeting. The major problem is to determine which organizations are ready. Next, it becomes critically necessary to understand the mechanism by which those organizations which aren't prepared can become prepared. Members of the Industrial Psychology Department at Vanderbilt University, for example, have developed a diagnostic questionnaire which assists in determining whether an organization is ready for rational strategic planning.

It was mentioned that the states of Colorado and Michigan and the Province of Ontario, Canada have implemented program budgeting systems.

In Ontario, each school's charter was removed and school representatives now appear before a board to justify their efforts.

IMPLEMENTATION OF FORMAL PLANNING

Problems of implementing formal planning techniques fall into five major categories: data, models, measures of effectiveness, human behavior, and politics. Several important questions were raised on the subject of implementation. For example: (1) Is there evidence that college campuses are poorly managed? (2) Would management improve if a particular model or information system were implemented? (3) What evidence would one look for to suggest improvement in management as a result of implementing a model? (4) What type of changes would one expect to see as a result of an effectively implemented model? In response to this latter question, the following items were mentioned:

a)   flows of relevant information would increase inside the organization;

b)   a more participative decision making environment would evolve (more staff involved in curriculum planning, for example);

c)   funds would begin moving toward more popular programs;

d)   changes in organization structure would be expected to occur with specific people responsible and accountable for specific programs.

Some models (e.g., student flow models) can be general enough to fit many institutions. Others have to be more customized. A number of institutions are presently using the RRPM model; several others now use CAMPUS.

The planning function during periods of growth in higher education is different from planning during periods of stability or decline. In the former situation, a major question is how to corner more resources for the long run. In the latter case, the question becomes one of how to immediately reallocate existing resources. Thus, systems analysts may be answering the wrong question first. Administrators need answers to give legislators *now*, not six months from now. Analysts, then, should learn how to give administrators what they need and want as soon as they ask. This seemingly is one answer to the question of how to gain support for planning techniques.

KEY QUESTIONS FOR PLANNERS AND DIRECTIONS FOR FUTURE RESEARCH

Before planning can be formalized within an educational environment, it seems appropriate that the planners attempt to answer some basic questions.

1.   What is the difference (if any) between education and training?

2.   Can and should the same people and institutions train and educate?

3.   Has the public been oversold on education?

4.   Is education being misrepresented to the consumer?

5.   Does higher education sell courses, degrees, and/or programs?

6.   Should institutions of higher education specialize?

7.   Is growth in Gross National Product caused by or merely related to education?

8.   Is a professional school (e.g., business school) a training institute and if so should it be marketed as such?

9.   Does the educational administrator have any power or right to administer his organization or is his position one of creating mechanisms whereby others can and do supply this leadership function?

10.   If we are moving toward vocational training, what methods of continuing certification will be used for those teachers in such professions as music, nursing, marketing, journalism, architecture, and so forth?

11.   Is education manageable?

12.   How many "Edsels" are being turned out by higher education?

13.   Would a voucher system work for higher education?

SOME IMPLEMENTATION STRATEGIES

Suggestions and comments were offered by participants as to those characteristics and problems related to implementing planning models in an institution of higher education. A summary of the discussion follows:

1.   Organization readiness. In order for a program budgeting system to work there must be a driving force with credibility; there must be enthusiastic, persistent support from the president and across all vice-presidential positions.

2.   There must be emphasis on decision making and the decision maker, and not on the tools.

3.   There should be an adequate data base within the organization, A good information system is necessary before modeling and program budgeting can be effective.

4.   There must be quantifiable output measures. Admittedly, it is difficult to quantify information which has traditionally been considered as qualitative. For example, one discussant pointed out that "protection of academic freedom" was given top priority among forty-seven goals as ranked by faculty, administrators, and students in a large university. The question is: how is this objective quantified or even rationalized?

5.   Goals and institutional philosophy should originate at the top of an organization. Generally, this does not happen in educational institutions. Change from the bottom up is slow and ardous. (Carnegie-Mellon proved

how fast change can occur when the top administrator is competent and willing to make hard decisions based on the best information available, according to one participant.)

6.   Decision makers who are too involved in day-to-day operating decisions have little time for planning. They tend to have very short time-horizons, whereas they should be allocating a certain percentage of their time to long run problems.

7.   Legislators must become informed in order that they may ask the right kinds of questions. Trustees, presidents, and planners should work as a team to communicate to the lawmakers.

8.   In a time of tight budgets, one of the first things to be down-graded is planning, just when it is needed most. Recognition must be given to the increased need for planning in "tough times."

9.   Program budgeting is thought to be primarily a top management tool by many who are uninformed about its usefulness at lower levels. Therefore, educational programs should be established for deans, chairmen, and faculty.

10.   Many program budgeting advocates attempt to put massive, total systems in all at once. Techniques are needed which can be used to do specific jobs almost immediately. Immediately useful and implemented techniques might help to solve the larger systems planning models. An example was provided of a linear programming algorithm used in the Tallmadge, Ohio, school district for allocating funds to various positions.

11.   Program directors should be active participants in the establishment of effectiveness measures for their particular programs.

12.   The Provincial Government of Ontario has experienced some success in implementing program budgeting, as was pointed out earlier. In this system one person with high credibility coordinates planning efforts for all schools. He circulates among the institutions discussing plans and results each year.

Those who claim the program budgeting concept is not working feel that a primary cause of failure is that systems people do not see the real world the same way that decision makers see it. They feel that many rational planning approaches neglect to incorporate political-social variables. Additionally, the systems analyst often greets the decision maker with a statement such as "I have a model which will provide rational planning for this institution." By implication, the systems specialist is saying that current decisions are not rational. Is there a faster way to turn off an administrator than by implying that he is irrational?

MEASURING OUTPUT OF HIGHER EDUCATION

The value of education is no longer taken for granted. No longer is it a "given" that education for education's sake is good. So how do you measure the value added by higher education?

Educational administrators and staff should be asked:

1.   Are you accomplishing anything (are you effective)? and

2.   Are you doing it efficiently?

If education doesn't like to be measured on these terms, then it is up to the educators to produce better measures. In any case, measures there must be. Numbers of students graduated or FTE enrollments are no longer sufficient measures of organization effectiveness.

Business has developed ways to measure consumer attitudes. Education might be able to adopt these techniques. In any case, multiple objective functions should be developed based upon "consumer" attitudes and needs.

It is the power bases within organizations which now determine which programs get cut. This process has nothing to do with a rational allocation of resources or a social preference order. Yet legislators must be supplied with ammunition which they can use to show the taxpayer what is being obtained for the dollars being spent.

CONCLUSIONS

Based on the discussion that occurred during the program budgeting and information systems workshop, the following conclusions are drawn by the authors:

1.   Technology can help universities to improve their planning efforts. This technology may or may not take the form of program budgeting.

2.   Rather than merely responding to special interest groups, university administrators have the responsibility and indeed the need for short and long range planning.

3.   Close surveillance over and reaction to product markets and consumer demands must be achieved.

4.   Program budgeting may be appropriate for some educational institutions, but it is probably not appropriate for all. There are indicators which help to determine whether an organizations is ready for such planning techniques.

5.   Educational administrators can use budget constraints to their favor or, as an alternative, be used by these constraints.

6.   Collective bargaining is going to gain power and influence in higher education. Administrators must be trained and willing to develop with this unionization since it will force greater flexibility and greater planning requirements.

7.   Planning through model building is expensive, especially if done by each institution independently. This is a major reason why an organization such as NCHEMS, which started in 1969 with ten western institutions, has over eight hundred cooperating members at the time of writing.

APPENDIX

Dr. Ian MacGregor, Vice President for Planning at the University of Akron, provided his feeling regarding the crisis of planning in higher education and his reactions to the conference. To the best of our ability, we quote him as follows:

I would like to give my reaction to this conference. Based upon what I have heard, it seems to me that administrators of universities have been eminently successful in getting new model builders and systems people to ask the right questions. I suppose it isn't working in the other direction. For the past two days you have been addressing the philosophic questions of the direction in which higher education is going. These are the kinds of questions systems people and modelers had better start asking themselves. Maybe the administrators have been successful in getting you to ask this kind of question.

Within any institution you must recognize that the president, the chancelor, the provost, or whoever is chief executive is *the* planning officer. He is charged with the responsibility of planning for the institution. The services that he can get from other departments are vital to him in making decisions. On this basis, his staff, including the planning officer, the vice president for academic affairs, the director of institutional research, the financial officer, and others can prepare recommendations for him. Using these recommendations, he must make the decision as to what will be recommended to the board of trustees, the state board of regents, or the state board of education. He has to make these decisions and have them approved before they can be implemented. Therefore, I urge all of you not to kid yourselves into thinking that faculty, other administrative offices, or students are making the decisions. When all is finished, the president has the responsibility and is charged with that responsibility from the beginning.

If faculty want to institute change, they must make recommendations to the president through appropriate channels based upon reason and logic. It is here that I feel the modeling and systems analysis people can be of great assistance. I'm not in agreement with some of you who have made the implication that administrators always feel that they are doing good, that they don't need or want data that models can give them, or that the system can give them. They want it alright! They might not know how to ask the questions and they may be afraid of the models, but these, I think, have to be worked out with the modelers and the administrators together. A lot of this depends upon organization and I'm glad to see that almost every group during this conference brought up the vital subject of organization for planning. Whether we talk about crisis planning, crisis reaction, or advanced planning, it depends upon a particular institution and probably upon the chief executive officer. But the institution must be organized for planning.

I realize there are many executive officers that feel no sympathy for planning or modeling simply because they don't understand it. On the other hand, we who are planners in some way or another may have failed to bring to their attention the things that models can provide. We must show that models can assist in setting priorities. We must assure that the models speak the language of the executive or that an interpretor is available to convert the language of the model into the language of the adminis- trator. In my own situation as a planning officer, I am very excited about opportunities that models provide. Models will give me either data or projections that I need and that are valuable to me as I deal with other vice presidents, deans, faculty, and students in discussing future programming. I recognize, however, that many of my recommendations are not going to be accepted.

The coming of faculty collective bargaining, whether you like it or not, will introduce new factors into models or change some of the old factors, and I hope that the planning, programming, budgeting people and the model builders are doing something with these factors—because this is the time to do it. What will the effect of collective bargaining be? What will happen to tenure rules? Will rules simply become a matter of seniority? What's going to happen to fringe benefits? What about parking? I personally believe that the data base and models will help administrators in the future to make better decisions. I believe that administrators will be influenced by models and systems in the process of being developed by you people at this particular time.

IMPACT OF THE CAMPUS MODEL ON DECISION PROCESSES IN THE ONTARIO COMMUNITY COLLEGES

Les Foreman
SDL Systems Research Group
Ontario, Canada

The CAMPUS model is not only a simulation model, it also provides a superstructure for the development of an information system in an educational institution. Most of the participants at this conference are probably familiar with the concepts of CAMPUS, if not the details of its operation Thus, this paper will concentrate on the information framework it provides and its effect on the management of the Ontario community colleges.

The CAMPUS version presently in use in Ontario is highly generalized. Many of the definitions and terms are determined by the input data. A considerable amount of data is required to drive the model, since it operates at a very detailed level. On one hand, this represents a sizable task. We believe it also represents a major advantage of CAMPUS VIII over other resource allocation models currently available in that it provides a simulation capability right down to the individual department and course level Virtually all the data required to operate CAMPUS are basic information which should be available in any institution with reasonably good records. CAMPUS provides a structure for the systematic organization and documentation of this information. In Ontario, where we are dealing with a system of colleges, this structure extends beyond individual institutions and produces information which is comparable and useful for system-wide analysis. Furthermore, it draws data together so that it provides information not known previously or in a significantly different and more understandable format.

Although data organization is an important function, CAMPUS would not merit the attention it has received if it did not do more. In fact, its simulation capability, supported by an extensive set of reports, make it a very powerful analytical tool. It is a very good approximation of the "reality" of the situation at a college. An experimental capability allows the administrator to alter the policies or variables in the system which are subject to change in the real world of the college. He is permitted to examine the effects of different decisions before he may actually have to live with these effects.

Ontario has a community college system made up of twenty-two colleges at sixty campuses. These colleges teach approximately 50,000 full-time equivalent day students and another 50,000 full-time equivalent manpower retraining students. The Council of Regents is responsible for the over-all coordination and planning for the system of colleges, and the Ministry of Colleges and Universities, a government department, acts as the secretariat for operational matters to the Council.

The management style of the colleges is such that the Council of Regents wishes to encourage a great deal of individual initiative on the part of the colleges, both with regard to their planning and management and their academic operations. At the same time, the Council has the responsibility for coordinating the request for the total operating and capital support of the colleges, on behalf of all of the colleges, to the Legislature in Ontario. In order to justify its case to the Legislature and ensure that the colleges are operating in a reasonably efficient and effective manner while maintaining a decentralized approach to management, the Council of Regents and the Ministry decided to promote the use of modern management techniques.

In 1969, a pilot project was carried out in three of the colleges to test the concept of implementing a coordinated approach to planning, budgeting, and reporting to the provincial and federal governments. The project involved the implementation of an early version of the CAMPUS simulation model in each of the colleges and the development of prototype computer-based reporting systems on students, staff, space, finance, and curriculum. Standard definitions of data elements, costing procedures, and program structures were developed, as well as procedures for the development of program oriented operating and capital budgets covering a five-year horizon. All of this was structured in such a way as to allow the colleges to pursue virtually any reasonable approach to academic programming.

The success of the pilot project led to a decision to implement the system on a full scale basis in 1970. This first year was mainly one of technical work, setting up internal procedures for data collection, establishing data bases, and further testing the technical systems and operations. In 1971, the system was put into full operation. The colleges used the CAMPUS system and its associated procedures to prepare five-year master plans covering academic, physical, and fiscal requirements, and the Province began carrying out all reporting, both for its purposes and those of the federal government, through the central data base. In addition, analytical programs for displaying information on the group of colleges were put in place. Last year (1972) represented the second year of full operation. All the colleges were required to submit a multi-year plan to the Council of Regents on March 1, 1973. The first year of the plan fulfills the Legislature requirement for an annual budget. These plans and associated analyses are public documents which will be presented to the Legislature in support of appropriations for the colleges. This will be a continuing process, with colleges submitting revised five-year plans every March.

Decision making in higher education is seldom a public activity. To the extent that it is, this process is not easily examined or measured. Figure 1 represents the organizational relationship in the Ontario system. SDL Systems Research Group interacts with all the organizations represented on this chart. The CAMPUS system acts as a continuing catalyst in the decision making process in those organizations.

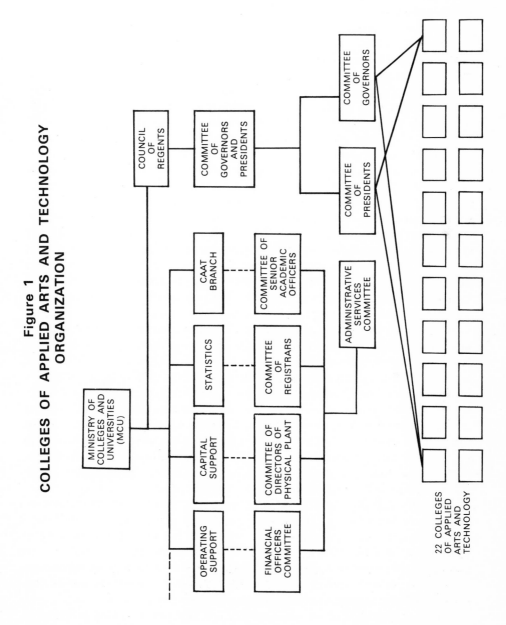

Figure 1
COLLEGES OF APPLIED ARTS AND TECHNOLOGY
ORGANIZATION

CAMPUS AS AN INFORMATION SYSTEM

It cannot be said that the path has always been a smooth one, nor is it yet. We met some strong resistance to our activities when the project first began. One of my earliest recollections is a conversation with a dean who told me that I represented what he disliked most in the Ontario education environment. By this, he said, he meant that it was the old problem of the tail wagging the dog. Instead of giving him a free hand to determine the educational program and providing the funds he requested, the Province was using the money to force a different pattern. He was at least partly right about me and my colleagues. There are a number of very legitimate competitors for public funds and it is not easy to decide between alternative pressures for scarce public resources. Education, as a result, is required increasingly to justify its requests for public funds.

This dean was not alone among staff members of the community colleges, especially the academics. But we also heard similar comments from some administrators. Subsequent experiences in other jurisdictions and circumstances lead me to believe that this attitude is widespread. However the opinion is expressed, the opposition is really directed against systematic planning. All of us have listened to statements like "I have no idea how many students will be taking this course (program, major, etc.) next year"; or "Nothing in our past experience prepares us for what will happen in the future"; or "Student demand is shifting so rapidly that it is impossible to forecast any trend"; and so on. Frequently such statements are just excuses for inaction or delaying the time when a decision must be made. The prevailing attitude seems to be one of just "leave us alone and things will work out alright." Planning is analyzing the long-term implications of present actions. Significant changes, therefore, can only be introduced over an extended period and must be thoroughly considered. If the attitudes described above are deeply embedded in the educational system, the role for planning and rational decision making may be in doubt. One of the most important services that WICHE has performed is the work it has done to publicize and encourage the use of modern management techniques in higher education. We support this activity and have tried to make all our systems compatible with the WICHE definitions and structures.

Another problem we faced was serious opposition to the idea that information should be gathered and made more generally available in the academic community. By the very nature of its data requirements and operations, the CAMPUS system brings together much more information than had previously been available; it also distributes it more widely. In retrospect, we see that we displayed naivete on this point. Not everyone believes that better and more available information promotes better decisions.

Perhaps we did not appreciate the extent to which knowledge is power. Some people interpreted our activities as a threat to their positions. Some were reluctant to reveal policies or data to which only they had been privy. Since CAMPUS includes data on the entire operation of the institution, a number of people must be the sources of information. Sometimes rivalries and power struggles became evident, as information hiding and/or hoarding took place. This problem was overcome gradually as staff members developed confidence that they would not be sidestepped and as they saw the real benefits of sharing information. Although CAMPUS does bring about centralization and coordination of information processing, it does not necessarily result in centralization of power. In fact, it allows decentralization of power since senior management can monitor performance without making all the decisions.

A related problem was the serious lack of reliable data (sometimes any data) in areas that we considered critical. For example, there were colleges that did not have records on class sizes, numbers of students in programs, faculty workloads, average salaries, numbers of classrooms and their utilization, and so on. Now decision making can take place in an information vacuum, but we believe that more effective decisions are made on the basis of facts and good data. In many circumstances these data were absent and the CAMPUS system has filled a very real void.

In spite of scattered objections, the Ministry of Colleges and Universities continued to support the CAMPUS project and it was continued. The data gathering and validation processes took somewhat longer than most of us had anticipated. Partly it was a result of underdeveloped or non-existent information systems at the colleges. Where this was the case, CAMPUS became the structure for internal college data systems. In a few cases deliberate obstruction appeared to be taking place. This may have been caused by a lack of understanding of the system's requirements, or bad data, or the attitudes toward information and planning described earlier. Some colleges also had real concerns about the manner in which the model performed some of the calculations and viewed the output with scepticism.

As all of you are aware, data collecting can be a dull, boring experience. When it has to be repeated a number of times for inexplicable reasons, it is also very frustrating. But we and some of the colleges began to realize that the "process is the product." The very exercise of examining the logic of the CAMPUS model and checking its data is a very fruitful activity irrespective of what the final output turns out to be. This is a very real intermediate benefit of the system. In may cases, decision making responsibilities became clarified. Sometimes new communication patterns were formed and increased information exchange almost always took place. The exercise may or may not have produced better decisions, but at least the decision makers were better informed. In a number of institutions new information came to light.

One example was a college in which an academic division decided unilateraly to change the program content and increase the student course load by almost 20 per cent. The program area is funded on the basis of average student contact hours and this decision had important financial ramifications. Unfortunately, neither the president nor the business officer were informed of the decision. It was not until the business officer was trying to validate the output data from CAMPUS that he discovered the anomaly. After some discussion, the decision was resubmitted through the appropriate channel in the college structure. Other examples are:

College A revised the length of the academic year after discovering that it was actually two weeks shorter than provincial requirements and four weeks less than the college calendar statement.

College B discovered that its actual teaching staff load was less than college policy and varied widely by department.

College C decided to build rather than lease its facilities after noting that it was obtaining poor utilization from its rented buildings. The CAMPUS system was used to justify the amount of new physical facilities to the provincial agency.

College D provided revised instructions to its architect on the mix of classroom sizes after reviewing CAMPUS output.

The problems we encountered in Ontario are neither unusual nor specific to computerized simulation models. They are really a function of two things. The first is relatively poorly developed data base or information retrieval system. Although this situation is improving generally, there are still major gaps in most post-secondary institutions. The second is a widespread set of attitudes towards planning and decision making. On the basis of our experience in Ontario, CAMPUS is structured to overcome both these problem areas.

CAMPUS AS AN ANALYTICAL TOOL AT THE COLLEGES

As indicated earlier, CAMPUS is more than a data base manager or an information retrieval system. By 1972, useful and valid information was being produced and used in all the colleges. This allowed the system to be exercised in three ways. The first is sharing comparable information between colleges. The multi-year plans are all public documents and are based on standardized input definitions. Second, a college can use the system to experiment with alternative modes of operation. Finally, a college is able to conduct internal program evaluation by using the output reports from CAMPUS.

CAMPUS is a resource allocation model which deals with the resource implications of changed conditions in an institution. All colleges made at least three different enrollment forecasts in the submission of their multi-year plans on March 1. Only the most probable one was submitted but the others are available on request by the Ministry. A number of colleges have been conducting other experiments as well.

Figure 2 is a summary of a series of experiments that have been done for one particular college. This school is projecting a budget deficit of 10 percent by 1974–75. These experiments were done at the rate of one a week in order to give the college officials a chance to examine and digest the results of each one. The decision making process is accelerated greatly and the administrators have much better information on which to base their decisions.

Several colleges recognized during the preparation of their multi-year plans that significant changes would be required in order to weather expected

Figure 2
COLLEGE-EXPERIMENTS

Experiment

Result

1. Reduce (or increase) contact hours in Post Secondary Programs to 26.6 per week.

   Little overall change resulted for the college as a Nhole. Within post-secondary program sub-categories the effects were noticeable. Where hours presently were more than 26.6, the deficit would decrease and vice versa.

2. Set all labs and field work at 1/2 teacher per section (for the whole college).

   The deficit was entirely eliminated for 1974 and almost eliminated for 1973. A large surplus in the Health Sciences division resulted.

3. Cut attrition for post-secondary programs in half.

   The deficit was cut by $350,000. Effect was particularly noticeable in Technology. But the surplus in the Health Science division has decreased. This must be looked into further.

4. Eliminate in 1973 and 1974 the eight programs with the lowest percent cost recovery, all under 75%, assuming that the students taking those programs would not attend the college.

   Total effect appears to be nil. That is, the decrease in operating cost was matched by a loss in formula financed income. However, if only the 3 programs with a 50% cost recovery are eliminated, there is a net decrease in the deficit.

financial storms. After reviewing the CAMPUS output, these colleges are consciously adopting new policy positions. Some specific examples are:

College A is exploring the possibility of changing its academic structure from three years of thirty weeks each to two years at forty weeks per year. The different ramifications are being studied with the CAMPUS model.

College B examined its present and future teaching space requirements. There had been considerable discussion between the administration and faculty about the need for more classroom space in the near future. This issue is now set at rest.

College C considered the choice between increasing section sizes or increasing teaching staff loads. The latter was found to be more expensive.

College D was able to use the CAMPUS reports to justify the phases of its building expansion program just before a capital moratorium was imposed.

College E is conducting a number of simulations to examine the impact of the worst conceivable situation next fall. It is being called the "disaster-year" experiment.

Figure 3

CAMPUS VIII
INSTITUTION —
LOCATION —

REPORT   MY09
MAR. 15/73   SHER
JOB
PAGE   2

PROGRAM COST AND INCOME SUMMARY
****

PROGRAM. 2—HOTEL & RESTAUR.

	ACADEMIC YEARS					
	1971/72	1972/73	1973/74	1974/75	1975/76	1976/77
TOTAL STUDENT CONTACT HOURS	52455	49453	61620	67284	73788	77460
TOTAL NUMBER OF COST FTE STUDENTS	61.57	58.04	72.32	78.97	86.61	90.92
STUDENT ENROLLMENT IN FIRST TERM	56	53	63	71	78	82
STUDENT CONTACT HOURS IN FIRST TERM	27165	21930	26700	29160	32010	33630
AVERAGE CONTACT HOUR LOAD/STUDENT IN FIRST TERM	465.09	413.77	410.77	410.70	410.38	410.12
TOTAL COST	152365	118391	140325	151388	179078	179783
COST PER STUDENT CONTACT HOUR	2.90	2.39	2.28	2.25	2.43	2.32
NUMBER OF FORMULA FTE STUDENTS	56.00	53.00	65.00	71.00	78.00	82.00
NUMBER OF ATU'S UNDER FORMULA	72.06	64.93	78.10	85.20	93.60	93.40
COST OF PORTION UNDER FORMULA	152365	118391	140325	151388	179078	179782
FORMULA INCOME	124456	114607	142534	158642	177746	196501
SURPLUS/DEFICIT OF PORTION UNDER FORMULA	−27709	−3784	2209	7234	−1332	10118
% COST RECOVERY OF PORTION UNDER FORMULA	81.81	96.80	101.57	104.79	99.26	106.02
INCOME PER FORMULA FTE STUDENT	2226	2162	2193	2234	2279	2324
COST PER FORMULA FTE STUDENT	2721	2234	2159	2132	2296	2192
INCOME PER BIU	1730	1765	1825	1862	1899	1937
COST PER BIU	2115	1823	1797	1777	1913	1827
COST AS A % OF TOTAL FOR WEIGHT CATEGORY 3	4.80	3.56	3.74	3.66	3.92	3.55
INCOME AS A % OF TOTAL FOR WEIGHT CATEGORY 3	3.88	3.66	3.99	3.96	4.01	3.86

TOTAL PROGRAM COSTS BREAKDOWN BY BUDGET FUNCTION

1 — ACADEMIC	92369.50	72719.00	86762.75	95308.94	119523.56	119609.50
2 — ADMINSTRTVE	29269.41	20119.20	24002.44	25286.94	27028.40	27327.79
3 — PLANT	23075.20	16009.65	18094.17	18599.71	19420.88	19392.95
4 — STUDENT SERV	31.02	3627.11	4456.09	4815.97	5236.81	5442.16
5 — EDUCAT. RES	7619.96	5916.28	7009.41	7376.56	7868.45	8010.33

PROGRAM TOTALS AS A % OF TOTALS FOR THE SUBCATEGORY 1—APPLIED ARTS

OPERATING COSTS	4.80	2.84	2.81	2.66	2.80	2.49
STUDENT CONTACT HOURS	4.79	3.04	3.10	3.00	3.00	2.86
COST FTE STUDENTS	4.79	3.04	3.10	3.00	3.00	2.86

PROGRAM TOTALS AS A % OF TOTALS FOR CATEGORY 1—POST SECOND

OPERATING COST	3.26	2.03	2.07	1.96	2.06	1.83
STUDENT CONTACT HOURS	3.33	2.21	2.32	2.25	2.23	2.11
COST FTE STUDENTS	3.33	2.21	2.32	2.25	2.23	2.11

College F is studying the effect of different program content and attrition rates over several years.

College G has imposed new policies in its academic area which gradually increase section sizes and teaching staff loads and decrease student course loads. The effect of these decisions should enable the college to avoid a deficit in the face of increasingly stringent funding rules.

There is a program costing method within the CAMPUS system which allows the distribution of the total operating cost to programs. Since it also calculates the revenue generated by the programs, it is possible to compare these two figures. Figure 3 is a page from the output reports. It describes a specific program offering. It contains a considerable amount of information that is of interest to administrators. A few items that are most relevant to this paper are underlined. Note that an administrator is given, for each of the six years, the total cost of the program, its revenue, the surplus or deficit, and its cost recovery ratio. An identical report is also available and provides this information for a group of programs or the institution as a whole.

These reports are supported by a number of more detailed reports which provide an "audit-trail" procedure to substantiate the numbers. Decision makers have now been provided with a tool which gives them an accurate and comprehensive analysis of the institution and its programs. Consequently, a number of the colleges have embarked on a thorough program review using these reports. The senior personnel are going through every program and asking hard questions about the objectives, viability, utility, and cost effectiveness of each one. There is a danger that this process could turn into a witch-hunt, but it has not happened so far. To some extent, this is attributable to the very detailed reports that back up the system. Departmental chairmen have been able to produce information quickly to support their positions, where they are defensible. The overall result has been a learning and communicating process for all levels in the colleges.

CAMPUS AT THE SYSTEM-WIDE LEVEL

The final level of decision making is that conducted by the central agency. In some respects, this is both the most interesting and least developed area. The provincial officials have always been the strongest supporters of the whole concept. This was true even earlier when the preliminary nature of the data weakened their usefulness at this level. The plans submitted by the colleges in March, 1973, have given the Ministry the opportunities it has been awaiting since the beginning of the project. It is too early to judge the impact on decision making at this level, but we can report on some interesting developments.

All publicly-supported post-secondary education in Ontario is financed on a formula basis. Each institution receives an operating grant based on the number of students enrolled in the current fiscal year. This system worked relatively well during the expanding years of the sixties. Some of the universities experienced a drop in enrollment last September and incurred serious budgetary shortfalls as a result. The crisis this caused in at least one university eventually led to the resignation of the president. Pressures to change the formula financing system began to build and it soon became evident that the Ontario government was going to respond. But the question was how. The CAMPUS model was used to examine a number of different alternatives for the community colleges. The information produced by these experiments and the multi-year plans was used extensively in the final decision that was made.

The other development is the analysis of the multi-year plans submitted by the colleges. When these plans are received by the Ministry, a team of officials reviews each one and prepares a fifteen-page summary. Figures 4, 5, and 6 are typical pages from these summaries for a specific college. The numbers shown are taken right off the reports from the CAMPUS system included in the multi-year plans. As you can see, these analyses provide very clear cost and income numbers for each institution. We also worked with the Ministry to provide average numbers for the whole system of colleges in the same format. These analyses are used by the central agency officials as a basis for discussing the multi-year plan with each college at a public meeting.

The last development is a set of reports that we have primarily produced for the central agency. This state-wide CAMPUS system uses the variables from the CAMPUS output reports (approximately 250), and displays the information in the format shown in Figures 7 and 8. The colleges can be grouped in any manner required and up to three different variables may be combined in a single report. This is a recent addition to our system and its usefulness is still being explored. Nevertheless, the information it displays is a first, at least in Ontario. We are not aware of other jurisdictions in which comparable data are available at this level of detail and on a system-wide basis. The provision of such data surely will have an important impact on decision making at the provincial level.

It is difficult to measure the impact of CAMPUS in clear, quantifiable terms. One important point to bear in mind is that the impact cannot be tested over a short time period. We have observed a clear progression over the three years that the project has been funded. Staff members who were once skeptical about the concept of simulation are now energetically using the model to examine alternatives. There has been a clear change in the attitudes of many college officials regarding the use of the system.

Other observable differences may also be noted.

The standardization imposed by the system enables groups of colleges to share more data and experiences.

Because consistent data element definitions and classifications are used, colleges are more willing to share information since they are confident that CAMPUS reports from various colleges are comparable.

Budgeting is increasingly being viewed as a long-range planning exercise rather than a short-term fund distribution system.

Figure 4

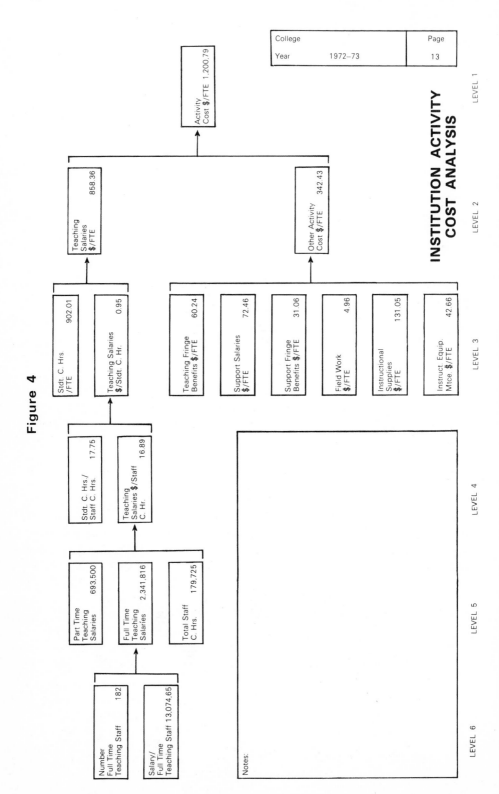

College		Page
Year	1972–73	13

**INSTITUTION ACTIVITY
COST ANALYSIS**

LEVEL 1

LEVEL 2

LEVEL 3

LEVEL 4

LEVEL 5

LEVEL 6

Figure 5

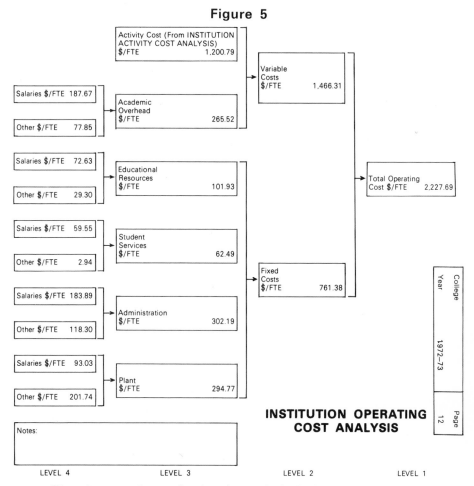

There is a growing realization that today's decisions have long-term implications.

Long-range planning and basic objectives are often input to the one-year budget process.

The open sharing of information has increased cooperation among colleges.

The provincial government is much better informed without having to centralize its activities and reduce the freedom of action and exercise of initiative at the colleges.

The CAMPUS system is indeed a superstructure for a complete management information system, as well as a very powerful analytical tool. Its role is to provide information to decision makers in the expectation that better decisions will result. If they are determined not to cooperate or use the information, the system cannot go much further. There are limits to the extent to which any external system can have impact on the decision making process. However, we have seen that it is possible to change attitudes with the passage of time. The decisions are thereby improved in that they are at least more fully thought out and rational.

Figure 6

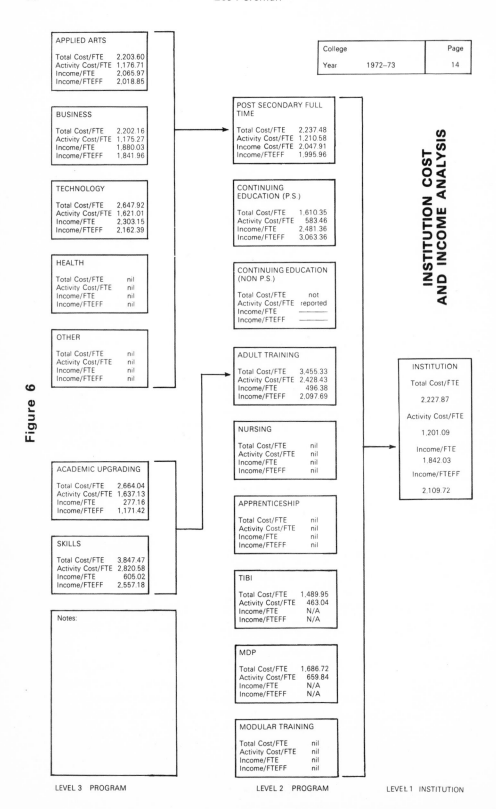

College		Page
Year	1972–73	14

APPLIED ARTS

Total Cost/FTE	2,203.60
Activity Cost/FTE	1,176.71
Income/FTE	2,065.97
Income/FTEFF	2,018.85

BUSINESS

Total Cost/FTE	2,202.16
Activity Cost/FTE	1,175.27
Income/FTE	1,880.03
Income/FTEFF	1,841.96

TECHNOLOGY

Total Cost/FTE	2,647.92
Activity Cost/FTE	1,621.01
Income/FTE	2,303.15
Income/FTEFF	2,162.39

HEALTH

Total Cost/FTE	nil
Activity Cost/FTE	nil
Income/FTE	nil
Income/FTEFF	nil

OTHER

Total Cost/FTE	nil
Activity Cost/FTE	nil
Income/FTE	nil
Income/FTEFF	nil

ACADEMIC UPGRADING

Total Cost/FTE	2,664.04
Activity Cost/FTE	1,637.13
Income/FTE	277.16
Income/FTEFF	1,171.42

SKILLS

Total Cost/FTE	3,847.47
Activity Cost/FTE	2,820.58
Income/FTE	605.02
Income/FTEFF	2,557.18

Notes:

POST SECONDARY FULL TIME

Total Cost/FTE	2,237.48
Activity Cost/FTE	1,210.58
Income Cost/FTE	2,047.91
Income/FTEFF	1,995.96

CONTINUING EDUCATION (P.S.)

Total Cost/FTE	1,610.35
Activity Cost/FTE	583.46
Income/FTE	2,481.36
Income/FTEFF	3,063.36

CONTINUING EDUCATION (NON P.S.)

Total Cost/FTE	not
Activity Cost/FTE	reported
Income/FTE	———
Income/FTEFF	———

ADULT TRAINING

Total Cost/FTE	3,455.33
Activity Cost/FTE	2,428.43
Income/FTE	496.38
Income/FTEFF	2,097.69

NURSING

Total Cost/FTE	nil
Activity Cost/FTE	nil
Income/FTE	nil
Income/FTEFF	nil

APPRENTICESHIP

Total Cost/FTE	nil
Activity Cost/FTE	nil
Income/FTE	nil
Income/FTEFF	nil

TIBI

Total Cost/FTE	1,489.95
Activity Cost/FTE	463.04
Income/FTE	N/A
Income/FTEFF	N/A

MDP

Total Cost/FTE	1,686.72
Activity Cost/FTE	659.84
Income/FTE	N/A
Income/FTEFF	N/A

MODULAR TRAINING

Total Cost/FTE	nil
Activity Cost/FTE	nil
Income/FTE	nil
Income/FTEFF	nil

INSTITUTION

Total Cost/FTE	2,227.87
Activity Cost/FTE	1,201.09
Income/FTE	1,842.03
Income/FTEFF	2,109.72

INSTITUTION COST AND INCOME ANALYSIS

LEVEL 3 PROGRAM   LEVEL 2 PROGRAM   LEVEL 1 INSTITUTION

Figure 7

CAMPUS VIII

MULTI-YEAR PLAN ANALYSIS

****

TOTAL OPERATING COSTS PER FTE

MAY. 08/73
COMB. 401
PAGE 1

	1971/72		BASE YEAR 1972/73	HIST%	PLANNING YEARS 1973/74	CUM%	1974/75	CUM%	1975/76	CUM%	1976/77	CUM%
ALL COLLEGES												
ALG	2196	*	2277	3.7	2320	1.9	2315	1.7	2448	7.5	2587	13.6
CAM	1958	*	2363	20.7	2337	-1.1	2437	3.1	2542	7.6	2646	12.0
CAN	0	*	2878	0.0	2903	0.9	3073	6.8	3286	14.2	3428	19.1
CEN	2297	*	2427	5.7	2551	5.1	2710	11.5	2837	16.9	2985	22.2
CON	2289	*	2406	5.1	2344	-2.6	2381	-1.0	2456	2.1	2694	7.8
CON	2809	*	2892	2.9	3150	8.9	3330	15.2	3485	20.5	3661	26.6
CUR	2450	*	2416	-1.4	2323	-3.9	2383	-1.4	2446	1.2	2522	4.4
FAN	1952	*	2240	14.7	2369	5.8	2433	8.7	2533	13.1	2615	16.8
GED	0	*	0	0.0	0	0.0	0	0.0	0	0.0	0	0.0
GEO	1909	*	2568	34.5	2613	1.8	2600	1.3	2559	-0.3	2570	0.1
HUM	2134	*	2194	2.8	2286	4.2	2367	7.9	2456	11.9	2590	18.0
LAM	2374	*	2556	7.7	2634	3.0	2679	4.8	2755	7.8	2841	11.1
LOY	2829	*	2761	-2.4	2839	2.8	3011	9.1	3188	15.5	3362	21.8
MOH	2075	*	2180	5.0	2201	1.0	2303	5.7	2418	11.0	2515	15.4
NIA	2392	*	2398	0.2	2455	2.4	2564	6.9	2682	11.9	2853	19.0
NOR	2750	*	3124	13.6	3171	1.5	3258	4.3	3374	8.0	3550	13.6
ST. C	2177	*	2407	10.6	2539	5.5	2793	16.2	3093	28.5	3366	39.8
ST. L	2036	*	2169	6.5	2345	8.1	2261	4.2	2294	5.3	2429	12.0
SAU	2323	*	2557	10.0	2577	0.8	2704	5.8	2872	12.3	3028	18.4
SEN	0	*	0	0.0	0	0.0	0	0.0	0	0.0	0	0.0
SHE	2532	*	2228	-12.0	2166	-2.8	2170	-2.6	2198	-1.3	2230	0.0
SIR	1985	*	2210	11.4	2282	3.3	2434	10.1	2578	16.6	2748	24.3

Figure 7 (*Contd.*)

CAMPUS VIII

MULTI-YEAR PLAN ANALYSIS
****

MAY.   08/73
COMB. 401
PAGE   1

TOTAL OPERATING
COSTS PER FTE

	1971/72		BASE YEAR 1972/73		PLANNING YEARS 1973/74		1974/75		1975/76		1976/77	
				HIST%		CUM%		CUM%		CUM%		CUM%
AVERAGE	2288	*	2463	7.6	*	2520	2.3	2611	6.0	2725	10.7	2855	15.9
WEIGHTED AVERAGE	2218	*	2358	6.3	*	2413	2.3	2484	5.3	2589	9.8	2709	14.9
MEDIAN	2289	*	2407	5.1	*	2412	0.2	2500	3.9	2569	6.7	2697	12.1

****

NOTE: "HIST%" USES 1971/72 AS THE BASE
        "CUM%" USES 1972/73 AS THE BASE

Figure 8

CAMPUS VIII

MULTI-YEAR PLAN ANALYSIS
****

MAY. 08/73
COMB. 402
PAGE 1

VARIABLE COSTS
PER FTE

	1971/72	BASE YEAR 1972/73	HIST%	PLANNING YEARS 1973/74	CUM%	1974/75	CUM%	1975/76	CUM%	1976/77	CUM%
ALL COLLEGES											
ALG	1641 *	1631 *	−0.6	1680	3.0	1694	3.8	1804	10.6	1918	17.6
CAM	1358 *	1584 *	16.6	1526	−3.7	1605	1.3	1690	6.7	1784	12.6
CAN	0 *	1761 *	0.0	1770	0.5	1894	7.5	2019	14.6	2116	20.2
CEN	1575 *	1671 *	6.1	1760	5.3	1899	13.6	1989	19.0	2097	25.5
CON	1628 *	1704 *	4.7	1661	−2.5	1702	−0.1	1771	3.9	1879	10.2
CON	1880 *	1854 *	−1.4	2025	9.2	2169	17.0	2296	23.8	2437	31.4
DUR	1580 *	1613 *	2.1	1620	0.5	1697	5.2	1764	9.4	1842	14.2
FAN	1398 *	1603 *	14.6	1757	9.6	1845	15.1	1957	22.1	2049	27.8
GED	0 *	0 *	0.0	0	0.0	0	0.0	0	0.0	0	0.0
GEO	1376 *	1725 *	25.3	1762	2.2	1802	4.4	1809	4.9	1846	7.0
HUM	1340 *	1357 *	1.3	1436	5.8	1517	11.8	1599	17.8	1705	25.6
LAM	1396 *	1522 *	9.0	1597	5.0	1653	8.7	1719	13.0	1792	17.8
LOY	1915 *	1888 *	−1.4	1904	0.8	2034	7.7	2164	14.6	2295	21.6
MOH	1433 *	1527 *	6.6	1647	7.9	1741	14.0	1843	20.7	1927	26.2
NIA	1594 *	1580 *	−0.9	1637	3.6	1734	9.7	1836	16.2	1968	24.6
NOR	1917 *	2186 *	14.0	2292	4.8	2427	11.0	2530	15.8	2680	22.6
ST. C	1470 *	1534 *	4.3	1599	4.2	1778	15.9	1976	28.8	2159	40.7
ST. L	1418 *	1485 *	4.7	1624	9.3	1587	6.9	1633	10.0	1734	16.8
SAU	1533 *	1677 *	9.4	1717	2.4	1825	8.8	1964	17.1	2089	24.6
SEN	0 *	0 *	0.0	0	0.0	0	0.0	0	0.0	0	0.0
SHE	1647 *	1466 *	−11.0	1452	−1.0	1486	1.3	1535	4.7	1589	8.4
SIR	1325 *	1488 *	12.3	1552	4.4	1684	13.2	1800	21.0	1926	29.5

Figure 8 (*Contd.*)

CAMPUS VIII

MULTI-YEAR PLAN ANALYSIS

VARIABLE COSTS
PER FTE

MAY. 08/73
COMB. 402
PAGE 1

	1971/72	BASE YEAR 1972/73	HIST%	1973/74	CUM%	1974/75	CUM%	1975/76	CUM%	1976/77	CUM%
						PLANNING YEARS					
AVERAGE	1549 *	1643 *	6.1	1701	3.5	1701	8.9	1789	14.7	1885	21.2
WEIGHTED AVERAGE	1520 *	1591 *	4.7	1656	4.1	1656	8.8	1731	14.7	1825	21.1
MEDIAN	1533 *	1608 *	4.9	1654	2.9	1654	8.1	1737	13.4	1822	19.8

NOTE: "HIST%" USES 1971/72 AS THE BASE
"CUM%" USES 1971/73 AS THE BASE

THE MINNESOTA AND COLORADO EXPERIENCES WITH THE CAMPUS PLANNING SYSTEMS

Gary M. Andrew and Madelyn D. Alexander
University of Colorado

The purpose of this paper is to discuss the aspects of implenting the CAMPUS model in Minnesota as Project PRIME, and in Colorado at the University of Colorado. The first place to start would be to define "implementation" as it was meant in Minnesota, and as it is meant today in Colorado. In Minnesota, Project PRIME (Planning Resources in Minnesota Education) was principally a research project to investigate the difficulties of implentation and the adaptability of the CAMPUS model, and to investigate two critical areas of the model itself—faculty activity analysis and program costing.

At the University of Colorado, implementation means making CAMPUS part of the planning and budgeting system, creating data systems which support an annual update of the data base, and communicating to the full range of users from the faculty to State officials so that maximum use is made of the model's capabilities.

With these definitions in mind, this paper will describe the objectives and accomplishments of these two projects. The disaggregate approach of CAMPUS makes it a difficult model to "bring up," since the data requirements are massive and detailed; but it is this very characteristic which creates two distinct advantages. The first serves the general management of an institution. The ability of the model to carry inventories of staff, space, activities (a component of a course, i.e., lab, lecture), students, and other resources (nonpersonnel costs) enables the model to set up relationships between and among the various data systems. It can serve facilities master planning and budget planning for reallocation. It can even serve in generating a factbook. It can do these things because of the comprehensiveness of the data which it can hold. This ability makes it a management information system in itself.

The second advantage of CAMPUS' detail is the distinctive manner in which CAMPUS can serve the planning process. Aggregate planning models can be very useful in planning a new institution or planning for the expansion of existing institutions. However, few of us are going to have the pleasure of working in such institutions in the next fifteen to twenty years. *A first principle* in institutional planning is that mature, stable institutions have many more constraints than young and/or growing institutions. Planning in mature institutions must fully recognize these constraints. The University of Colorado at Boulder *is* a mature institution that has reached its enrollment limitation (20,000 FTE students). Hence, total enrollment, one of the biggest variables that drives aggregate planning models, is a constant and only change in mix within the given total enrollment is variable. In such a situation, more detailed information is necessary. (It is generally true that any decision making under constraints requires more data than without constraints.)

A result of these constraints is that change in a mature institution is much slower than in a growing institution. *A second planning principle* is that it is extremely important to understand the time transformations that can take place and convert a constraint at one point in time into a control in a longer time horizon. For example, next year there may be little or no flexibility in the faculty complement, while in a five-year horizon, turnover and retirements may allow new choices of personnel and new directions for the department. This results in the need to better understand the total operation of the system as it *is* and identify those constraints in the current system that can be changed through a longer time (planning) horizon.

A third principle of planning in higher education, which we try to follow, is that planning should be a continuum from the most disaggregate organizational unit (the department or division), all the way through central administration, and on to whatever state coordination takes place. This continuum must be a two-way communication channel and decision process.

Given these three principles, it is important that any planning system in a mature institution give sufficient detail so that the intricacies between constraints and control variables and time are understood, and that the system provide information along the continuum from the most disaggregate unit to the most aggregate level of planning. This philosophy dictates that the planning function must be intimately familiar with the operations of the institution and that the operations must be involved in planning.

When evaluated against these criteria, most of the existing operational planning models fail. The disaggregate approach of the CAMPUS model is necessary to satisfy the criteria. This advantage of the dissaggregate model has the additional effect of flexibility to report data in the PCS structure, the State budget structure, the internal organization structure, and in the student program* structure. This multiple reporting allows for an expanded base of communication.

Each of the implementation projects has addressed five major areas:
(1)   Software conversion aspects of the model
(2)   Data collection and linkage with operating data systems
(3)   Training/Communications
(4)   Research

At Minnesota, CAMPUS V was *converted* from the software on an IBM 360/65 to the CDC 6600. After this conversion was completed, a costing module was added to the software of the CDC 6600. At Colorado, CAMPUS VI was purchased from SRG and was redesigned jointly by SRG and the University of Colorado. The redesign was of a major nature. It included program costing as well as student program costing. It included the ability to add computational relationships for resource planning and an expanded

---

*A student program is defined as a student emphasis (major) which leads to a degree, certificate, or some other stated objective.

list of bases (or variables) to be included in these relationships. This redesign was accomplished first and then the conversion of IBM 360/65 software to CDC 6400 was done.

Data gathering at Minnesota was done in an *ad hoc* manner. There were no long-range plans for maintenance. The units modelled were small; hence, data collection could be done by hand. In Minnesota, the staff was very familiar with the units and validation was done "by eye." At Colorado, the goal was different. Data will have to be collected each year to update the base case data (the base year of each simulation). Validation in Colorado had to be rigorously built-in because of the size and complexity of the institution, and because validation procedures should be independent of the staff's knowledge of the organization being modelled. As a result, extensive design was done to develop software which extracted data from the operating data systems of the University. This also served to reduce the "collection" task at a large campus, such as Boulder. This approach has created a much slower implementation, but one which will allow for update on a continuous basis.

The *training program* used in Minnesota was extensive. Approximately twenty seminars were given throughout the year and served to acquaint the higher education community with the capacity and uses of CAMPUS. Again, a long-range approach has been taken at Colorado. Only initial seminars have been given to top-level administrators, deans, and certain state-wide groups. However, an extensive program has been developed which will be implemented in the second year of implementation. This program is designed to develop users of the model. Seminars will be directed to department chairpersons, faculty policy committees, nonacademic department heads, and, again, to deans.

Project PRIME was a *research* project. Its primary objective was to investigate. As a result, it supported two extensive research projects, along with the testing of implementation. Faculty activity analysis and costing aglorithms were thoroughly examined. These are reported elsewhere (Lorents, 1971; Cordes 1970). At Colorado, it has not been possible to do any significant state-of-the-art research. With emphasis on long-range procedural aspects, research has been postponed.

The objectives of the Minnesota project did not support the incorporation of CAMPUS into an *on-going planning* and *budgeting system*. At Colorado, this has been the ultimate objective. The entire implementation has been designed so that the repetitive parts become a part of the operating systems, eventually leaving time for the staff to work on the interface with users and significant research problems. In addition, the CAMPUS reports are being slowly incorporated into the budget system. At the present time, it is predicted that even the State will use CAMPUS as the budget presentation medium. This coverage from the department level to the State will give strong incentive to incorporate and use CAMPUS in the entire planning and budgeting system.

In Minnesota, the intricacies and problems of implementing CAMPUS at three different types of institutions was examined. Each institution was "brought up" and simulation experiments were done. At the University of Colorado, the model has been running at the Colorado Springs campus and is now being used extensively in master planning. At the Boulder and Denver campuses, the first module of CAMPUS has been run and these data, though limited, are already being used by planning groups across each campus (Andrew, 1973). Total implementation and absorption into the operation of the University is seen to be one to two years in the future.

REFERENCES

Alexander, Madelyn D.
  1973   *The Implementation of CAMPUS/COLORADO at the University of Colorado.* Boulder, Colorado: University of Colorado. Paper to be presented at the AIR 1973 Annual Conference in Vancouver, British Columbia, Canada. To be published in the proceedings of that meeting.
Alexander, Madelyn D.
  1973   *The Implementation of CAMPUS/COLORADO: Boulder, Colorado Springs, Denver, Progress Report No. 1.* Boulder, Colorado: University of Colorado. January.
Andrew, Gary M.
  1973   *CAMPUS at Colorado.* Presented at SCUP 1973 Spring Conference, "Let's End the Confusion about Cost-Simulation Models!" Washington, D. C. To be published in the proceedings of that meeting.
Andrew, Gary M.
  1973   *Academic Planning—Using a Cost Simulation Model for Structuring Information and Communication.* Boulder, Colorado: University of Colorado. (Draft.)
Andrew, Gary M., David C. Cordes, and Alden C. Lorents.
  1971   *Project PRIME Report No. 14, Mid-Year Report.* January.
Andrew, Gary M., David C. Cordes, and Alden C. Lorents
  1971   *Project PRIME Report No. 16, Final Report: Project PRIME.* Minnesota Higher Education Coordinating Commission. July.
Cordes, David C.
  1970   *Project PRIME Report No. 2, An Introduction to Project PRIME and CAMPUS MINNESOTA.* November.
Cordes, David C.
  1971   *Resource Analysis Modelling in Higher Education: A Synthesis.* Unpublished Ph.D. Dissertation. University of Minnesota, School of Business Administration.
Lorents, Alden C.
  1971   *Faculty Activity Analysis and Planning Models in Higher Education.* Unpublished Ph.D. Dissertation. University of Minnesota, School of Business Administration.
Mason, Thomas R.
  1973   *The Purpose of Analytical Models: The Perspective of Model User.* Boulder, Colorado: University of Colorado. Presented at SCUP 1973 Spring Conference, "Let's End the Confusion about Cost Simulation Models;" Washington, D.C. To be published in the proceedings of that meeting.

A FEDERAL PLANNING MODEL FOR ANALYSIS OF ACCESSIBILITY TO HIGHER EDUCATION: AN OVERVIEW[*][+]

Vaughn E. Huckfeldt
National Center for Higher Education Management Systems
Western Interstate Commission for Higher Education

INTRODUCTION

Under a National Planning Model project contract from USOE, the National Center for Higher Education Management Systems (NCHEMS) has developed a prototype higher education model for the analysis of the impact of alternative financing plans on accessibility to higher education and institutional viability (the ability of institutions to meet explicit institutional goals with a given level and mix of federal aid). The basic purpose of the National Planning Model project is to provide an initial prototype higher education model that would permit prototype planning studies to demonstrate the feasibility of such analytical tools for national policy analysis of higher education, and that would also assist in identifying high-payoff areas for further research needed to develop a comprehensive national planning model.

This report presents a review of where the National Planning Model project fits in the process of developing improved analytic tools at the federal level. An overview of the prototype model is presented in nontechnical terms, followed by example reports from the model and a description of other related project reports.

ONE STEP TOWARD A NATIONAL PLANNING MODEL

The National Planning Model project undertaken by NCHEMS is one step in the development of analytic tools which will assist USOE's Office of Planning, Budgeting, and Evaluation in answering questions such as, "Will basic opportunity grants or general institutional aid have the greatest impact on achieving the national goals in higher education?" There are a

---

[*] This report is part of a research program supported by the Department of Health, Education, and Welfare, Contract No. OEC–O–72–3575. Ideas and opinions expressed in this paper are those of the author and do not necessarily reflect an official position of NCHEMS, WICHE, or the U.S. Office of Education.

[+] This paper was originally published in 1973 by the National Center for Higher Education Management Systems at Western Interstate Commission for Higher Education. The editor wishes to express appreciation to the NCHEMS for its permission to reproduce this material.

number of areas in which it would be desirable to measure the impact of alternative funding patterns, including:

1. student access to various types of higher education;

2. the viability of various types of postsecondary institutions (that is, the ability of the institutions to meet explicit institutional goals with a given level and mix of federal aid);

3. national manpower production;

4. the amount and quality of research;

5. the quality of education.

A comprehensive National Planning Model would provide a simultaneous analysis in all of these areas, but limitations on modeling techniques, data availability, and the available resources have necessarily limited the scope of the present study. Student access to higher education was selected as the initial area to be studied. This initial effort is only one step in the direction of a comprehensive National Planning Model for Higher Education. This phase of the project has produced an operational prototype Federal Model for Analysis of Accessibility to Higher Education which:

1. is based on existing derivable institutional and student data;

2. permits prototype planning studies to examine the impact of alternative federal programs on accessibility and, to a lesser extent, on institutional viability;

3. assists in identifying high-payoff areas of research necessary to develop a comprehensive National Planning Model and the additional data requirements of such a model.

MODEL CONCEPTS AND DESIGN

A general overview of the concepts and design of the prototype model is presented in this section. To facilitate a better understanding of the computations performed in the Federal Model for Analysis of Accessibility of Higher Education, a set of examples of the computations is presented in the Appendix.

The role of the federal government in higher education in the United States is, for the most part, indirect. The federal government, with few exceptions, does not operate or directly control higher education institutions. Neither, with few exceptions, does it decide which students will and will not participate in higher education, nor does it direct students to particular institutions. Rather, the federal government has an impact on higher education through various general and categorical financial aid programs for institutions and through many forms of student aid. The federal government does not fiscally dominate American higher education; it provides approximately 10 per cent of the total resources devoted to institutions and students. Individual states and private sources collectively bear the major costs and make the majority of the financing decisions. However, the federal role is significant because it is the largest single financial supporter of higher education and the only public agent with national responsibilities.

In order to investigate the impact of federal educational programs, it is necessary to examine the complex pattern of interaction between state governments, federal governments, institutions, and individuals. This problem will be approached by first, examining each of these components that influence or are part of the educational system, and then second, by considering the interrelationships that exist between the components. This examination begins with the actual education aspects of each of the components of the system shown in Figure 1 and then follows with an explanation of the way the prototype model simulates or attempts to duplicate that component.

The components related to the higher education system, as shown in Figure 1, illustrate the indirect role of the government in providing financing incentives to institutions and students. The resulting actions taken by the institutions and students in satisfying their own objectives are illustrated by the interaction of the institutional supply of student spaces and the student demand for spaces, which results in the current enrollment in higher education. The components to be examined are the federal programs, state programs, environment, institutions, and individual students.

Federal Government

The indirect nature of the educational influence of the federal government has already been mentioned. These federal actions take place when Congress establishes various institutional or student aid programs. The federal agencies then establish guidelines and administer the aid programs. The federal aid programs may be general in nature, like developing institutions aid, or may be categorical, like facilities aid.

An example of the combination of funding programs providing part of one of the current alternative funding packages is shown in Figure 2. A comprehensive summary of funding programs would include over 300 different programs.*

How, then, is this conglomeration of federal programs placed in the model? As shown in Figure 3, the prototype model does not attempt to identify each of the separate federal aid programs specifically. Rather, a set of generic types of federal aid has been established. Federal aid to institutions is included in the model by establishing the following generic types of aid: federal construction aid per assignable square feet (ASF) of space built, federal construction aid per student, federal general aid. The financial incentives the federal government offers to individuals for attending higher education are grouped into federal grants to students and federal loans to students. Both the grant and loan categories are subdivided into income and ability quartiles for different socioeconomic groups in the population. The

---

*According to a study by the National Financing Commission.

Figure 1
COMPONENTS OF HIGHER EDUCATION

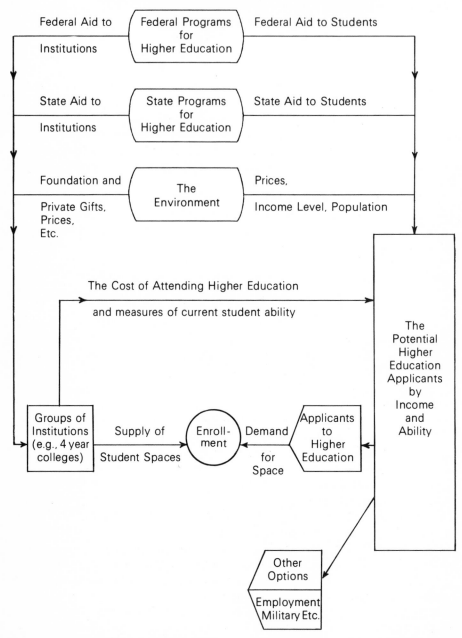

federal aid that is disbursed by the states is included in the institutional or student aid in the prototype model.

State Governments

State governments (see Figure 4) establish many institutional and student aid programs using a variety of legislative methods and organizational

Figure 2
THE FEDERAL CONTRIBUTIONS TO HIGHER EDUCATION

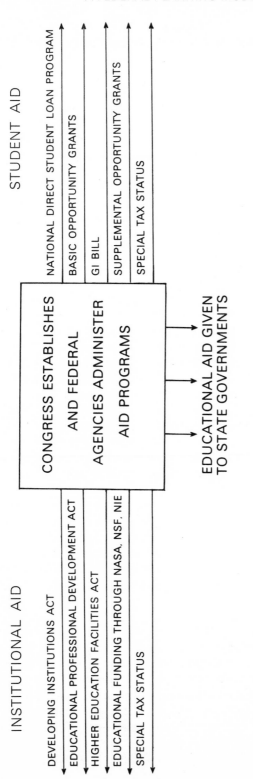

Figure 3
THE FEDERAL COMPONENT OF THE PROTOTYPE MODEL

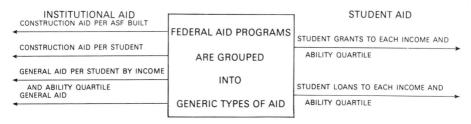

structures.* The state governments also function as disbursing agents for a certain portion of the federal dollars which come to the states as dollar matching grants or through revenue sharing. The interrelationship between the federal and state dollars is a complex set of decisions that are dependent upon many of the other state-wide financial demands (transportation, health welfare, environment, and so forth).

Typical state methods of allocating educational dollars to institutions include legislative allocations to line item budgets, categorical grants for facilities, general appropriations for coordinating councils or boards, and various forms of formula budgeting in which the budget is a function of items such as full-time students, credit hours, or degrees granted. The state student aid programs are typified by such programs as the regents scholarships, for example, of the State of New York. Other state student aid programs may develop as a result of future federal dollars being allocated to states with requirements that these dollars go directly to students.

As shown in Figure 5, the state governments are grouped into one unit in the prototype model. The prototype model is currently designed to look at the overall impact of alternative federal funding programs and not to provide specific state or regional information about the impact on higher education in a particular area of the country. The prototype model considers only the disbursing of generic types of the aggregated state higher educational dollars. State aid to institutions is categorized by: state construction aid per ASF built, construction aid per student, general aid per student, and general aid. The prototype model does not currently include state aid directly to students, but this is one of the first additions that should be made when sufficient data are available.

The Environment

To discuss all of the elements of the environment that have an effect on higher education is not possible in an overview report. Figure 6 simply illustrates several of the main environmental elements, such as industrial support, foundation grants and private gifts, general prices in the economy, rate of inflation, average yearly income, interest rates, current population, and the availability of employment and other alternatives to higher education.

---

*A complete review of the statewide educational structures is found in *Higher Education in the States*, Vol. 2, No. 4, May 1971.

Figure 4
THE STATES' CONTRIBUTIONS TO HIGHER EDUCATION

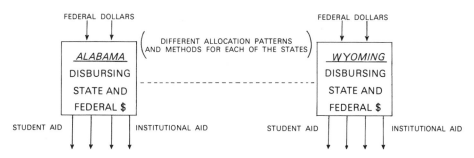

Figure 5
THE STATE COMPONENT OF THE PROTOTYPE MODEL

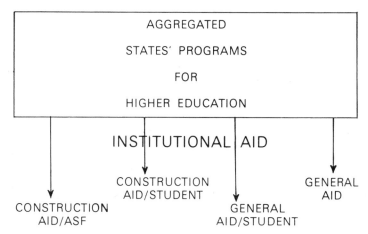

Figure 6
THE ENVIRONMENTAL INPUTS TO HIGHER EDUCATION

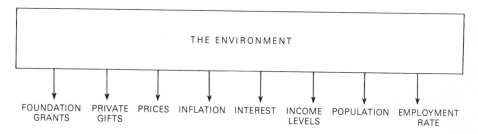

Figure 7 illustrates the elements of the environment that are included in the prototype model. The support is classified into unrestricted additions to endowments and restricted additions to endowments. Prices are included by using average prices, for example, the average price of construction cost per ASF built. Average interest rates are included in the cost of capital funds

Figure 7
THE ENVIRONMENT COMPONENT OF THE
PROTOTYPE MODEL

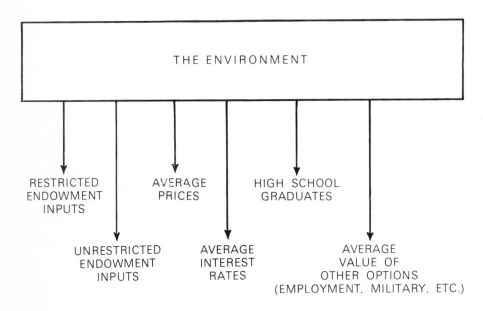

financed, but inflation is not currently included in the prototype model. The population that may potentially enter higher education in the coming years is taken to be the predicted number of high school graduates, and their income level is specified as an average income for a given income quartile. The employment opportunities are simulated by considering the average economic value of selecting other options (business, military, government, unemployment, etc.) rather than attending higher education.

Institutions
     There are more than 2600 higher education institutions in the United States. A comprehensive description of these institutions would consider the programmatic structure of the institutions, the primary programs of instruction, research and public service, and the secondary support programs (Gulko, 1972). Through this programmatic structure the institutions combine the components shown in Figure 8 (faculty, facilities, students, and finances) to achieve certain institutional goals and objectives. With 2600 institutions, over 300,000 faculty members of different ranks, over 700 million square feet of space of various types, over 9 million students, and annual budget expenditures of over 25 billion dollars, it is easy to see that individual institutions cannot be the components in the prototype model.
     In the prototype model the institutions are categorized into groups of similar institutions, as shown in Table 1. The categories used are basically those of the Carnegie Commission, with the addition of the groups of developing institutions. Each of the groups of institutions is described by the aggregate numbers of faculty by four ranks, facilities by two types, students by three levels (lower division, upper division, and graduate), several

Figure 8
AN INSITITUTIONAL GROUP IN THE PROTOTYPE MODEL

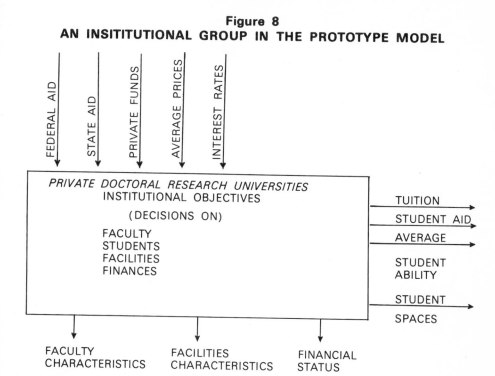

accounting funds, and a representation of the institutional goals and objectives. The relationships among these elements of the institutional groups are included in the prototype model by considering the decisions made by institutions as to the faculty to hire, the space to build, the students to admit, the tuition to charge, the student aid to grant, and the collective financial consequences of the decisions. The resource allocation decisions made in the prototype model for each group of similar institutions do not consider programmatic decisions allocating resources to specific programs of instruction, research, or public service. Thus the prototype model cannot evaluate specific funding programs that allocate aid to a type of program, and the prototype model cannot evaluate the manpower generated by specific programs. However, it can consider the simplest version of manpower, the total number of graduates by type of institution.

Individual Students. The relationships between individuals and higher education are of two types: those individuals who are currently students in the system and those individuals who are the potential applicants to higher education. The individuals who are already students are considered as part of the institution. In examining the accessibility of higher education to individuals, a model could take account of the fact that many socioeconomic characteristics can have an effect on an individual's decision to become an applicant to higher education. Among these characteristics are income, ability, age, sex, race, geographic location, previous educational attainment, individual goals and objectives, and peer group opinion.

Table 1
LIST OF GROUPS OF INSTITUTIONS USED IN THE MODEL

1. Developing Two-Year Public Institutions
2. Public Two-Year Institutions
3. Private Two-Year Institutions
4. Developing Public Universities or Colleges
5. Developing Private Universities or Colleges
6. Public Liberal Arts Institutions
7. Private Liberal Arts Institutions
8. Highly Selective Private Liberal Arts Institutions
9. Public Comprehensive Colleges
10. Private Comprehensive Colleges
11. Public Doctoral Research Universities
12. Private Doctoral Research Universities

In the prototype model, the potential applicants to higher education are classified into quartiles of income and quartiles of ability. While it would be desirable to include several of the other characteristics, they are omitted because of data unavailability, the increased dimensions of including them, and the fact that research has shown income and ability to be the significant components in an individual's decision about higher education (Miller, 1971). The current prototype model considers only the new potential applicants to higher education (high school graduates) and not those seeking continuing education later in life. This can easily be expanded to a broader class of potential applicants on the availability of improved data.

Component Interrelationships

In Figure 9, the interrelationships among the major components of the prototype model are illustrated. The user of the prototype model specifies (see box 1 in Figure 9) several years of the federal educational policies to be evaluated and specifies (boxes 2 and 3) the level of state programs, prices, population, and so forth to be held constant while varying federal policies. This enables the prototype model to separate the probable effects on student access over time that are induced by changes in federal programs from those induced by state programs or environmental factors. In response to these external financial incentives and consistent with their own internal goals and objectives, the institutions determine (box 4) a multiyear operating plan. This multiyear plan is simulated by calculating the numbers of faculty, square feet of space, students, and dollars based on average continuation rates for faculty, depreciation rates for space, and dropout rates for students. The multiyear capability permits the investigation of effects that occur over time as a result of changes in federal policies. From the multiyear institutional plan, the cost of attending a specific group of institutions (e.g., four-year colleges), and the average ability of students in the institutional group is determined. The prototype model next considers the possibilities open to individuals (box 5) as they choose the type of institution they will attend. The individuals consider for each type of institution the cost of attending, the aid available to students, the makeup of the student body, and their own individual ability and income. Then, cognizant of alternative options (box 6) in employment, the military, and elsewhere, the individual may actively seek admission to a particular type of institution (box 7).

Figure 9
A FEDERAL MODEL OF ACCESS TO HIGHER EDUCATION

Information about the impact of federal programs

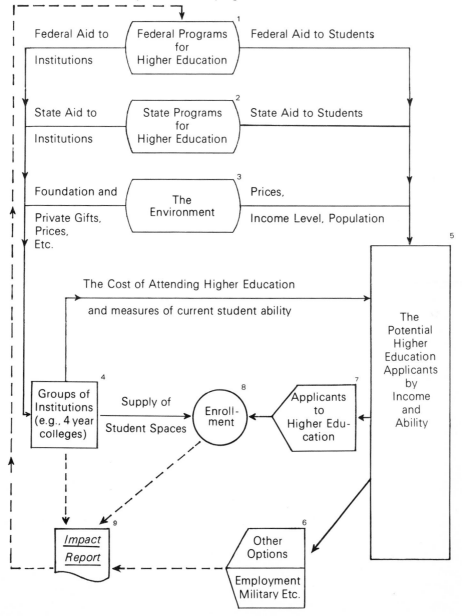

The model next combines the institutional spaces available, or the supply of education as determined from the institutional component of the model, with the demand for education as determined by the students selecting particular institutional types. This supply-and-demand interaction specifies the enrollment (box 8) to higher education, from which it is possible to determine the following: (1) the general level of enrollment in each type of institution; (2) the number of empty spaces in each type of institution; (3) the income and ability level of incoming students; and (4) the income and ability of persons who are not currently being served by higher education. Thus, each combination of alternative financing plans produces interactions among the students, institutions, states, and the federal government, resulting in an impact on accessibility and institutional viability. This impact report (box 9) can then be used by the federal policy analyst to adjust the federal education policies until results consistent with federal goals and objectives are obtained.

EXAMPLE REPORTS

The vast quantities of information available from the model would include:

1. Federal aid dollars by type of institution, general type of aid, and year in which the aid was used.

2. Institutional data on faculty by level, space by type of space, accounting statements for each type of funds, students for each income/ability quartile and level of student, and the number of empty spaces in the institution for each type of institution.

3. Student data on the number of applicants desiring entry to higher education, the number enrolling for the first time, and the number not entering higher education, all separated into income and ability quartiles.

Obviously, a report containing all of the above information for two alternative federal financing plans would be too detailed for effective use by a policy analyst. The first comparison of two plans should be made using summary reports, followed by an examination of more detailed reports as necessary.

One of the summary reports prepared for use with the model is shown in Figure 10, which may help in delineating the types of information the prototype model can provide. Consider an analysis of the following two alternative financing plans:

FINANCING PLAN 1
In addition to the current financing for higher education, add a $100 student voucher for every low-income-quartile student attending a higher education institution.

FINANCING PLAN 2

In addition to the current financing for higher education, add $100 of general institutional aid for every low-income-quartile student admitted to a higher education institution.

From Figure 10 it is seen that Plan 1 results in the admission of more students, while Plan 2 results in a higher net cash balance for the institutions and increased numbers of faculty. While this is necessarily a hypothetical evaluation of two plans, it does illustrate the types of comparisons that could be made with the model.

Figure 10
SUMMARY OF INSTITUTIONAL STATISTICS

NOTE

> *This report is presented as an illustration of the information the model can provide. The data presented in this report is hypothetical data and does not represent actual results of comparisons of the two financing plans.*

****PLAN 1—SUMMARY OF 1974 INSTITUTIONAL STATISTICS—
(in Thousands)

	Net Cash Balance	Total Faculty	Total ASF Space	Total Students	Federal Dollars	Cost Per Student
PUBLIC UNIV	247,322	103.1	268,224	2,354	1,020,769	2.5
PUBLIC 4-YR	87,071	64.2	152,613	2,178	214,925	1.1
PUBLIC 2-YR	46,710	31.1	96,460	2,503	17,254	1.1
PRIVATE UNIV	84,643	38.2	94,500	706	718,774	4.6
PRIVATE 4-YR	126,164	64.2	123,806	1,339	522,310	1.4
PRIVATE 2-YR	3,779	5.5	11,250	119	4,262	2.4
—TOTAL—	586,689	306.3	746,853	9,199	2,498,294	1.8

****PLAN 2—SUMMARY OF 1974 INSTITUTIONAL STATISTICS—
(in Thousands)

	Net Cash Balance	Total Faculty	Total ASF Space	Total Students	Federal Dollars	Cost Per Student
PUBLIC UNIV	273,155	107.4	268,440	2,105	1,025,243	2.7
PUBLIC 4-YR	92,721	66.2	152,658	2,156	216,969	1.2
PUBLIC 2-YR	74,308	35.4	96,510	2,485	23,300	1.1
PRIVATE UNIV	92,175	42.3	94,327	688	721,254	4.7
PRIVATE 4-YR	143,643	71.2	123,744	1,274	520,250	2.4
PRIVATE 2-YR	11,205	5.9	11,113	107	4,341	1.9
—TOTAL—	687,207	328.1	746,842	8,815	2,511,357	2.0

DESCRIPTION OF OTHER RELATED REPORTS

Additional information related to the results of this research effort can be obtained from other National Planning Model-Phase II project reports. A listing of all of the project reports would include:

1. *A Federal Planning Model for Analysis of Accessibility to Higher Education: An Overview.* A summary document that presents a discussion of the prototype model in nontechnical terms such that the basic concepts can be understood by the higher education community. This includes a set of example calculations to illustrate the computations in the model.

2. *A Design for a Federal Planning Model for Analysis of Accessibility to Higher Education.* A documentation of the assumptions, design considerations, detailed prototype model relationships, and possible future research. This includes the most detailed explanation currently available for the prototype model.

3. *Prototype Software for a Federal Planning Model for Analysis of Accessibility to Higher Education.* A complete listing of the prototype software for:

   a. MODIFY—a routine that creates or updates the data base for the prototype model.

   b. NPM 2.4—the current version of the prototype model.

   c. VIEW—output report routine that displays several summary reports from runs of the model comparing two alternative financing plans.

4. *Preliminary Operating Instructions for a Federal Planning Model for Analysis of Accessibility to Higher Education.* A report that presents very preliminary instructions for using the current prototype model software. This report is not a general user's manual as it does require extensive knowledge of the model and the software. However, it does provide an initial set of instructions that can be used with the prototype and a basis for an improved user's manual in the future.

5. *Preliminary Data for a Federal Planning Model for Analysis of Accessibility to Higher Education.* A preliminary report to illustrate the types of data used in preliminary tests of the prototype model. This report contains all of the prototype data values, descriptions of each variable, and the current source of the data.

6. *Preliminary Test Reports from a Federal Planning Model for Analysis of Accessibility to Higher Education.* A complete set of the current output reports illustrating the current operational status of the prototype model. Included are the summary output reports comparing two alternative financing plans and a complete step-by-step report of the status of the model at a number of intermediate checkpoints in the model operation. The step-by-step report includes both a simulation run of the institutional sector of the model and a segment of an optimization run illustrating improvements in objective function values.

All of the above reports should be considered preliminary reports on the National Planning Models effort by NCHEMS. These reports should and will be updated and revised extensively as and if NCHEMS is able to further develop the model.

REFERENCES

Education Commission of the States.
1971   *Higher Education in the States.* Legal Composition of State Coordinating or Governing Agencies and Public Institutional Governing Boards. Denver, Colorado: 2:4.

Gulko, Warren.
1972   *Program Classification Structure.* Technical Report No. 27. Boulder, Colorado: NCHEMS at WICHE.

Jewett, James E.
1972   *College Adminissions Planning: Use of a Student Segmentation Model.* Berkeley, California: Ford Foundation Program for Research in University Administration.

Miller, Leonard S.
1971   *Demand for Higher Education in the United States.* Presented at the Conference on Education as an Industry. Stony Brook, New York.

Wagner, Gary W., and George B. Weathersby.
1972   *Optimality in College Planning: A Control Theoretic Approach.* Berkeley, California: Ford Foundation Program for Research in University Administration.

APPENDIX
EXAMPLE MODEL COMPUTATIONS

To facilitate a better understanding of the computations performed in the Federal Model for Analysis of Access to Higher Education, a set of examples of the computations is presented in this section. In order to keep the calculations simple and emphasize the concepts rather than the arithmetic, the data used are simple hypothetical data and not necessarily representative of the real world.

The sequence of examples follows the general logic flow of the model. For simplicity, assume only one type of federal and state institutional aid (general institutional assistance). Given that the state level of funding is $1,000,000, let us consider the impact of a federal plan of $400,000 of institutional aid and $50 of direct aid to each student. Assume the calculation of the best five-year plan for the two-year institutional group has been completed and start with the calculations for the four-year institutional group. To keep the dimensions of the problem reduced to a feasible visual display, the example calculations will show one type of faculty (rather than four, as used in the model), one type of space (rather than two), one ability level (SAT = 600) and one income level ($10,000) of students (rather than four quartiles of income and four quartiles of ability), one general operating fund (rather than several accounting funds), and a one-year institutional planning horizon (rather than five years as in the model). The model starts the four-year institutional calculations by using as input data the current state of the institutional group in terms of the current number of faculty, students, assignable square feet, and current operating fund dollars. To these values the model adds institutional decision values such as faculty to hire, space to build, students to admit, and tuition to charge according to a base-year operating plan called Plan I. The values resulting from these calculations for the four-year institutional group show the state of the institution one year later if it used Plan I. The calculations are illustrated in Figure A-1. The number of variables in each of these calculations is greatly expanded in the actual model, but the example does give a feeling for the first set of calculations.

The statement of changes in the operating fund resulting from the Plan I decisions is shown in Table A-1. The list of items included in the full statement of changes includes student aid, administrative cost, physical plan operations, and federal and state aid separated into several categories. The state and federal components of the model appear as dollar inputs to the financial statement of the institution.

Table A–1
OPERATING FUND STATEMENT OF CHANGES

Net Cash Balance Carried Forward From Last Year	$520,000
ADDITIONS	
Tuition Revenue (Tuition × Total Students) $300 × 1400	$420,000
State Aid	$1,000,000
Federal Aid	$400,000
DEDUCTIONS	
Faculty Salary (Average Salary × Total Faculty) $10,000 × 110	$1,100,000
Construction Cost (Cost per ASF × ASF Built) $20 × 42,000	$840,000
Net Cash Balance Forward to Next Year	$400,000

The next step in the model is to consider the planning parameters of this group of institutions. The planning parameters, desired level for each parameter, and current level of each parameter (assuming the Plan I decisions) are shown in Figure A-2. The institution desires to have a student-faculty

Figure A–1

THE FLOW OF FACULTY, SPACE, AND STUDENTS

Next Year	=	Transition Value	×	This Year	+	Transition Value	×	Decision Variable
Faculty in FTE	98 =	.90 Continuation Rate	×	100 Current Faculty	+	.80 Continuation Rate	×	10 Faculty Hired
Space in ASF	140,000 =	.98 (2% Depreciation rate)	×	100,000 Current Space	+	1.0 (No Depreciation)	×	42,000 ASF Space Built
Students in FTE	1,000 =	.80 Continuation Rate	×	1,000 Current Students	+	.50 Continuation Rate	×	400 Students Admitted

Vaughn E. Huckfeldt

Figure A–2
THE INSTITUTIONAL PLANNING PARAMETERS

Planning Parameter	Desired Level	Current Level (Plan I)		
Students ——————— Ratio Faculty	15 — 1	Total Students ———————— Total Faculty	$\dfrac{1400}{110} = \dfrac{12.7}{1}$	
Tuition — Desired Target Tuition	250	Tuition — Target = $300 — $250 = 50		
Net Cash Balance	$200,000			$400,000

ratio of 15 to 1, while Plan I will result in a ratio of 12.7 to 1. The second planning parameter is to control the tuition level to $250, but the current plan has tuition set at $300. The last example parameter shown is for the net cash balance to equal $200,000, while Plan I will result in a $400,000 balance.

Since a number of the planning parameters calculated with current data are different from the desired levels, the model selects a better set of decision values to come as close as possible to the desired levels (Wagner and Weathersby, 1972). The new decision variable values for this alternative operating plan (Plan II) and the desired and realized planning parameter values are shown in Figure A-3.

Figure A–3
ALTERNATIVE OPERATING PLANS

Decision Variable	Plan I Decision Value	Plan II Decision Value	Planning Parameter	Desired Level	Plan I Level	Plan II Level
Faculty Hired	10	0	Students ——————— Faculty	15 — 1	12.7 — 1	14 — 1
ASF Space Built	42,000	53,500	Net Cash Balance	$200,000	$400,000	$200,000
Students Admitted	400	400	Tuition — Desired Tuition	0	50	0
Tuition	$300	$250				

This is the process of finding the alternative decision variable values that come closest to meeting the desired levels for the planning parameters. This process is then repeated for all of the other groups of institutions.

The model then calculates the apparent cost to the student of attending each group of institutions. In this example we are using only one student type, while in the model these student calculations would be repeated for each of the 16 student income and ability classifications. In these calculations, the apparent net cost to the student of attending an institution consists of tuition, plus a general cost of living, minus student aid received. For the students considered in the example institution, the general cost of living is assumed to be $1200, and the federal student aid policy being examined is assumed to be $50. Then:

$$\text{Net Cost} = \text{Tuition} + \text{Living Cost} - \text{Student Aid}$$
$$1400 = 250 + 1200 - 50$$

All of the information from this group of four-year institutions which will be needed in the student sector of the model is summarized as follows:

$$\text{Supply of Student Spaces} = 400$$
$$\text{Average Total Student Ability, SAT} = 600$$
$$\text{Net Student Cost} = \$1400$$

Note that the federal financing plan being considered ($400,000 institutional aid and $50 per student) has entered into the institution's decision proces in setting the supply of spaces at 400, and in the net student cost through tuition levels and student aid. The model now turns to the student sector and first calculates the number of potential postsecondary applicants by income and ability, as shown in Figure A-4. To carry out the example calculations, we will trace the calculations through the student sector using an ability level of SAT = 600 and an income level of $10,000.

The model then calculates a probability that the 15,000 potential applicants will attend a given group of institutions. Consider the following data for two different groups of institutions and for the alternative of selecting employment, the military, or other options:

	Net Cost	Average Ability of Student in this Group
Group of two-year institutions	$ 700	500
Group of four-year institutions	$1400	600
Other options (employment, . . .)	0	400

To calculate the three probabilities that the 15,000 potential students will attend the three choices, the model first calculates a value of attending each of the choices following a formula developed by Miller (1971). The actual constants in the formula were developed from historical student data. Remember, we are using the average applicant SAT = 600 and income = $10,000.

$$\text{Value of attending} = \text{Constant} \times \frac{\text{Net Cost}}{\text{Income}} + \text{Constant} \times \frac{\text{Group Average Ability} \times \text{Applicant Average Ability}}{1000}$$

Figure A-4
DISTRIBUTION OF APPLICANTS BY INCOME AND ABILITY

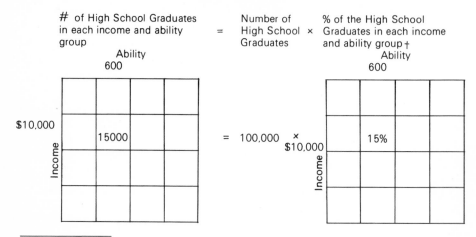

+Jewett, J. E., *College Admissions Planning: Use of a Student Segmentation Model*, Berkeley, California: Ford Foundation Program for Research in University Administration, 1971.

Value of attending two-year group of institutions $= .28 = -4.6 \times \dfrac{\$700}{\$10,000} + 0.02 \times \dfrac{500 \times 600}{1000}$

Value of attending four-year group of institutions $= .076 = -4.6 \times \dfrac{\$1,400}{\$10,000} + 0.02 \times \dfrac{600 \times 600}{1000}$

Value of other options $= 4.8 = -4.6 \times \dfrac{0}{\$10,000} + 0.02 \times \dfrac{400 \times 600}{1000}$

Then the probability of applying to any group of institutions is obtained by comparing its value to the value of attending all of the groups or selecting other options (i.e., employment, military, etc.). The actual formula in the model uses an exponential form, $e^{(value)}$, but the following calculations illustrate the concept:

Probability of applying to the four-year group of institutions $=$

$$\frac{\text{Value of attending the four-year institutions}}{\begin{array}{c}\text{Value of attending} \\ \text{two-year group of} \\ \text{institutions}\end{array} + \begin{array}{c}\text{Value of attending} \\ \text{four-year group of} \\ \text{institutions}\end{array} + \begin{array}{c}\text{Value of other} \\ \text{options}\end{array}}$$

$$.015 = \frac{.076}{.28 + .076 + 4.8}$$

The next step for the model is to multiply the probability of applying to the four-year group of institutions (.015) times the 15,000 potential applicants. Thus,

$$\begin{array}{ccccc} \text{Number of} \\ \text{Applicants} \end{array} = \begin{array}{c} \text{Probability} \\ \text{of applying} \end{array} \times \begin{array}{c} \text{Potential} \\ \text{Applicants} \end{array}$$

$$225 \quad = \quad .015 \quad \times \quad 15,000$$

Since the number of students the four-year institutional group desired to admit (the supply of spaces) was 400, all 225 applicants are admitted and the model calculates,

Empty spaces in four-year institutions = #Desired − #of Applicants

$$175 \qquad\qquad\qquad = \quad 400 \quad - \qquad 225$$

If the number of applicants were greater than the number the group desired to admit, the difference would then be expressed as unsatisfied student demand. When the model has completed this matching process for each of the 12 groups of institutions, the information on students, faculty, space, and finances can be obtained for each group of institutions. This evaluative information can be used to judge the impact of the selected federal programs being analyzed. The model uses the concluding data for the first federal planning year as a base and can run a sequence of yearly plans, each building on the results of the previous calculations.

THE EFFECTIVENESS OF SIMULATION MODELS IN ACADEMIC ADMINISTRATION

Robert F. Krampf and Albert C. Heinlein
Kent State University

Increased pressures on colleges and universities from students, faculty, and public are forcing a search for more effective and efficient administrative procedures. To assist these organizations in determining objectives, allocating resources, and general planning, various methodologies are being developed and utilized. These include mathematical modeling, information systems, and simulation models. This paper reviews the development and implementation of simulation models in colleges and universities. It is based on the round table discussions on simulation in academic administration held during the 1973 Decision Sciences Conference at Kent State University. Two simulation models, CAMPUS and RRPM, are looked at in some detail. Discussion then turns to the consideration of cost factors, data base requirements, actual usage, advantages and dangers of simulation models, and future research possibilities.

TWO SIMULATION MODELS: CAMPUS AND RRPM

Several simulation models[1] for academic administration have been developed at various universities throughout the U.S. and Canada. The most renowned simulation models are RRPM (Resource Requirement Prediction Model) and CAMPUS (Comprehensive Analytical Method for Planning in University Systems). The various comments directed at these models will be summarized here in an attempt to provide some information on the similarities and differences between them.

RRPM has been developed by NCHEMS (National Center for Higher Education Management Systems) at WICHE (Western Interstate Commission on Higher Education). Using data inputs, such as enrollment projections, course demands, support costs, salaries, and various academic and physical constraints, RRPM generates reports for one to ten years in the future. These reports include space requirements by department, student loads by student level and course level, cost per credit hour by department, etc. It is primarily a cost simulation that calculates the costs associated with a set of academic

---

[1] Besides the two discussed in this paper there are a number of others. Three of the better known among them are SEARCH (Systems for Evaluating Alternative Resource Commitments to Higher Education). The University of Minnesota Model, and The Michigan State University Model.

programs and the resources required to operate them. The model is also capable of responding to "what if" questions, indicating the effects of policy changes.[2]

CAMPUS, developed by SRG (Systems Research Group), now a subsidiary of SDL, provides more detailed output and can be implemented at various levels within the institution depending upon how much specific data the user wants to accumulate. It is possible to obtain individual department or course level information if desired. For a specific program within a college or department, it is possible to obtain student enrollment, cost per student, total student contact hours, teaching salaries on a dollar per student credit hour basis, etc. As with RRPM, it is possible to alter policies or variables in the system which are often changed in actual situations and observe the effects of different decisions.[3]

MBASIM, a small scale simulation model developed at Kent State University for generating and testing class schedules in the MBA program, provided an example of a modular approach to simulation in academic administration.

IMPLEMENTATION OF CAMPUS AND RRPM

One strategy that an institution might pursue in integrating simulation models into the decision making process would be to first implement RRPM and then follow with CAMPUS. Implementation in this manner would not result in a great loss of time or resources. RRPM is much quicker to implement (perhaps six months), but the data base employed would be useful and valuable in CAMPUS because the input data for both models have many similarities. CAMPUS requires considerably more technical support and a longer period of time to operationalize. It is possible to secure an RRPM program deck from NCHEMS for approximately $50.00 and to install it with existing staff. CAMPUS costs substantially more, in addition to requiring a technical support staff.[4] Because of the greater commitment required for CAMPUS and the relatively inadequate condition of many university information systems, RRPM may be a more reasonable first effort in simulation modeling for academic institutions.

It should be emphasized that data systems should not be built for the specific purpose of utilizing CAMPUS or RRPM. Rather, they should be constructed such that information necessary to run CAMPUS or RRPM can be derived from the broader data base. The data system should be completely operational before attempting to use it in a simulation model.

---

[2] For a more detailed discussion of RRPM see, *Introduction to the Resource Requirements Prediction Model 1.6*, Technical Report 34A (Boulder, Colorado: National Center for Higher Education Management Systems at WICHE, 1973).

[3] For a more detailed discussion of CAMPUS see, Richard W. Judy and Jack Blevine, *A New Tool for Educational Administrators: A Report to the Commission on the Financing of Higher Education* (Toronto, Canada: University of Toronto Press, 1965). This was published for the Association of Universities and Colleges of Canada.

[4] CAMPUS does provide more extensive and detailed output than RRPM. SRG-SDL provides the user with a great deal of help in implementing the simulation program.

The interface established with the faculty while implementing RRPM would be very valuable when expanding to the CAMPUS model. Both models require information from faculty. The communication system established to secure this information would be transferable from one model to another.

COST OF UTILIZING SIMULATIONS IN ACADEMIC ADMINISTRATION

It is not inexpensive to develop the expertise associated with RRPM and CAMPUS. To formulate the logic and code, and to debug and make programs operable, requires many man-hours. One participant stated that it took approximately eight years to develop its simulation model. The cost of adapting or redesigning existing simulation models is also significant. However, implementation of existing models, such as RRPM or CAMPUS, is much less expensive than developing new ones. Even the cost of running the simulation after it is installed is not negligible. Several examples will illustrate these operating costs.

CAMPUS can be run at a medium size institution (20 departments, 40 majors, 4,000 students, $10 million budget) for approximately $300. For this amount, one can obtain a complete five-year simulation with a full set of analyses and all reports. For a smaller institution (2000 students and other variables proportionately smaller), the cost would be $150–$200, while for a major educational institution (approximately 15,000–20,000 students), the cost would be in the neighborhood of $1000. The run cost goes up at approximately an exponential rate with enrollment. The above costs are almost entirely computer costs and do not include the expense associated with developing any portion of the required data base. (A more complete discussion of the development of data files and information system required to run a simulation will be presented in the next section.)

Due to the high cost of initial development, institutions are likely to find it desirable to utilize and adapt existing models rather than develop their own. Most of the available models are quite general and contain almost all the critical variables that one may wish to consider. Generally, terminology, reports, and alternatives are defined and described in accompanying reports.

DATA BASE REQUIREMENTS AND DEVELOPMENT

Considerable discussion evolved around the data base required to utilize simulation models. There were divergent views on this topic. Some contended that the utilization of simulation models improved the decision making process primarily by forcing the development of improved data systems. They held that decision making is often delayed due to lack of appropriate information. When a simulation model is implemented, the data base by necessity becomes more complete. Information is developed which is more appropriate to the decisions which must be made. With "better information," the administrator can (potentially) make better decisions.

Some agreed that improved decision making results from better information, but felt that data gathering and data base development were the only immediate benefits of simulation models. Furthermore, they felt requisite information could be obtained at considerably less cost when not associated with the requirements of a simulation model.

Others presented a compromise view. The data base is definitely an important starting point. But utilization of the model will yield even better decisions after administrators understand and trust it. One individual related that from his experience, if often takes several years to get to the point where the administrator has an adequate data base and has confidence in the reliability of the information provided. Only after confidence has been established are they interested in observing the effects of changes upon the system. Stopping with the data base is stopping short of the overall goal of improved decision making. A data base is constructed in order to describe what is presently happening in the institution. With simulation models, the decision maker is capable of exercising some sort of mathematical skill to examine the impact of different kinds of decisions on the future operation of the institution. Rather than a descriptive data set, he has a predictive model of the organization with which to study the effects of policy changes on the performance of the institution. Consequently, the decision maker can investigate problem areas that are too complex to analyze on his own.

USAGE OF SIMULATION MODELS

A favorable attitude on the part of administrators is the most important determinant of model use. Delay in implementation, which occurs both in business and academia, has been due primarily to lack of knowledge and understanding, communications failure, and general resistence to change.

There seems to be rapidly increasing interest in simulation models. This newly aroused interest results from the current urgent need for better decisions and an increased belief that simulation models can help meet the need.

A number of educational institutions have built simulation models into their information systems, but few are effectively using them as an integral part of the decision making process. Typical of this situation is an eastern university which recently implemented RRPM but whose administrators are not as yet using it in their decision making process. Among the institutions which have implemented simulation models are: the University of Colorado, the University of Toronto, Stanford, the State University of New York, Wheaton College, Thomas Moore College, and the University of Minnesota.

When the question was raised whether simulation models were actually utilized, many affirmative responses were provided. However, their responses were qualified in the sense that participants hesitated to say that they had observed total effective use of the simulation models.

ADVANTAGES AND DANGERS OF SIMULATION

Simulation models have a number of favorable attributes which academic institutions can use.

1. They force administrators to think more formally about the decision that must be made, thus imposing a definite logic upon the decision maker.

2. Simulation models preserve the administrator's autonomy for he still performs his main function of decision maker.

3. They allow the decision maker to ask "what if" questions so that he may study the implications of alternative policy changes within the institution.

4. Simulation models sometimes bring administrators "down to earth" regarding what they believe will happen if they continue to do what they are currently doing.

In spite of these favorable attributes a number of dangers and criticisms of simulation models were expressed during the discussion.

1. Users often try to extract too much from output generated by a simulation model. For example, if model results are not used in the sense of providing only "ball park" figures with which one can start to operate, erroneous conclusions can result since the detailed output is a function of roughly estimated inputs. Misusing the data in this manner is a frequent error.

2. Information often breeds the desire for more information to such an extent that it increases the time it takes to make a decision.

3. The information desired might be obtainable at considerably less cost without building a simulation model.

4. It is too mechanistic.

5. A great deal of data is required, hence entailing an extensive information retrieval system.

6. Decision makers may fail to realize that simulation is an aid to decision making, not a decision maker.

FUTURE RESEARCH

A number of areas exist for additional research in the development of simulation models.

1. Most simulations require some type of faculty effort analysis as input into the model. That is, it must be known how much effort faculty expend on classroom teaching, laboratories, research, committees, etc. This is a critical input since faculty expenses are a significant portion of total university budgets. Methods must be developed to obtain this information effectively and efficiently.

2. There is a need to look at the induced course load matrix that reflects course consumption patterns. Are they really as stable as is usually assumed? Can efficient methods be devised to develop a dynamic ICLM?

3. What types of relationships exist among variables that are part of the models? For example, what are the relationships between number of sections and requirements of supplies and equipment? In general, what relationship exists between any pair of columns in the data base?

4. How does the cost of a management information system with an associated simulation model compare with the cost of a MIS without a simulation model? Considerable discussion centered aroung this topic (as indicated earlier in this paper) but no empirical research could be cited to support either position.

5. Some felt that there was a need for research regarding duties and job requirements of university administrators and the information they require in order to make decisions for which they have authority. This information could be used to assess present models and develop future models.

6. There is a need to devise an operational method for measuring the output of higher education.

7. Investigations of the reasons for lack of implementation and utilization of simulation models in academic administration are needed.

8. The possibility of combining mathematical programming and simulation in order to develop more effective and comprehensive models of administration should be studied. For example, it was suggested that when one of the modules of CAMPUS deals with an assignment type problem, mathematical programming might be an appropriate tool.

In conclusion, there appear to be a considerable number of areas for continued research into the application of decision sciences to academic administration. Furthermore, students and faculty interested in this research field have available to them their own university as a laboratory to test their theories and ideas. Many refinements of the current modeling efforts are necessary. These can provide valuable inputs to colleges and universities attempting to implement and use models as an integral part of their decision making process.

A RESOURCE ALLOCATION AND PLANNING MODEL FOR HIGHER EDUCATION*+

Robert A. Wallhaus
National Center for Higher Education Management Systems
Western Interstate Commission for Higher Education

Long-range planning in higher education is a multistep process involving many individuals and perspectives. It is an iterative process that involves reformulation and experimentation. Planning in higher education should encompass a specification of objectives, an identification of programs for attaining these objectives, an examination of the associated resource implications, and then a reiteration of these steps to converge progressively on the best set of activities and resources in the context of the specified objectives.

Planning in the instructional area involves setting objectives that are usually quantitatively specified in the form of degree outputs. Formulating these objectives is itself a difficult and complex task, and at this point, the models developed in this paper become applicable. The linear programming formulations presented can be useful tools for evaluating alternatives and studying the resource effects, and can aid in investigating variations in objectives once indicators of instructional objectives are specified in the form of degree outputs.

USE OF SIMULATION MODELS IN HIGHER EDUCATION PLANNING

Simulation models, such as the NCHEMS-Resource Requirements Prediction Model (RRPM-1), can be of significant aid to the institution in determining the resource implications of alternative policy, operational, and planning changes (Gulko, 1971). Use of a simulation model may consist of experimenting with changes in operating policy (i.e., different class sizes, staffing ratios, salary schedules, etc.), investigating the results of changes in the mix and number of students, or expanding/curtailing institutional

---

*This study is part of a research program supported by the Ford Foundation, Grant Number 700–0434. Ideas and opinions expressed in this paper are those of the author and do not necessarily reflect an official position of NCHEMS, WICHE, or the Ford Foundation.

+This paper was originally published in 1971 by the National Center for Higher Education Management Systems at Western Interstate Commission for Higher Education. The editor wishes to express appreciation to the NCHEMS for its permission to reproduce this material.

programs. Such changes are simulated over time, thus yielding information relative to the resource implications of the various planning alternatives attempted.

While RRPM-1 in its present form is a valuable tool for long-range planning, it has a number of drawbacks, some of which will be overcome in future versions. These deficiencies of simulation models in general have been documented elsewhere (Breneman, 1969; Hopkins, 1969), but could be broadly classified into two categories:

1. Inaccurate Reflection of Reality—The model does not produce results that are consistent with what actually happens, perhaps due to invalid linearity or stability assumptions, a level of aggregation that clouds certain significant variables, misrepresentation of trends over time, omission of programs that have significant cost implications, and so forth.

2. Ease and Value of Experimentation—The value of the planning information produced by using the model, relative to the cost and effort required to run the model, needs improvement, perhaps because the output reports are inadequate in content, presentation, or overwhelming volume; computer requirements are large in terms of both run time and storage; the input preparations are burdensome and complex; the sequential mode of the simulation prohibits investigating many alternatives; etc.

Future versions of RRPM should be able to overcome a number of deficiencies in these areas without completely reconstituting the basic structure and computer programs. It is questionable, however, whether significant strides can be made in overcoming many of these defects by continually refining RRPM as a cost simulation model. Further, a particular conceptual difficulty with RRPM-1, the necessity to base experiments on *input* modifications, is inconsistent with a sound planning process. A decision maker should instead have the capability of investigating the resource implications of *output* alternatives; but this would be difficult, if not impossible, to achieve utilizing the traditional cost simulation approach.

While the model presented in this paper does not overcome all the objections that have been leveled at simulation models (and indeed, RRPM-1 will perform better in certain instances), the degree-goal planning model developed here does incorporate the following improvements:

1. It permits many planning alternatives to be investigated with little or no additional effort once an initial run has been made. The model allows a great deal of flexibility to experiment with different sets of degree output specifications. Limitations on transfers, variations in admissions, and different sets of available resources can be studied with small incremental computational costs once the initial solution is obtained.

2. The model is oriented toward investigation of the resource require-
    ments resulting from degree output specifications.

3. Underutilized resources are readily identified, as is an indication
    of an expansion path for adding resources within the context of
    minimizing deviations from stated degree production objectives.

While these advantages represent significant improvements over the
cost simulation approach, it should be recognized at the outset that the
model contains a number of limitations. These deficiencies are discussed
as the various aspects of the model are developed.

THE DEGREE GOAL PLANNING MODEL

The objective of the model is to come as close as possible to a *specified*
long-range plan for the degree output of an institution. The specified number
of degrees to be produced over time represents a planning alternative and,
therefore, an experiment in the simulation sense. The model is formulated
in a goal programming format, thus classical linear programming solution
procedures are applicable.

Let X_{kst} = number of students in degree program k, at level of
                    student s during time period t. (The usual choice for t
                    will be academic periods—semester, quarter, etc.)

a_{ijks} = element of the induced course load matrix—the credit
                    hour load on discipline i, course level j induced by
                    students in field of study (curriculum) k, at level s.
                    (Assumes stability over time.)

C_{ijr} = number of units of resource type r required per credit
                    hour in discipline i at course level j.

μ_{itr} = number of units of resource r available in discipline
                    i during time period t.

A_{kt} = beginning freshmen admissions into degree program
                    k at time t.

$P_{q,k,s,n}$ = proportion of students at level s in field of study q that
                    will be in field k at level n during the next time period.
                    (Assumes these probabilities are *not* a function of time.)

—*The constraints on available resources are:*
$$\sum_{j} \sum_{s} \sum_{k} C_{ijr}\, a_{ijks}\, X_{kst} \leq \mu_{itr} \qquad \text{(all i, r, and t} >1) \quad (1)$$

—*The constraints on Student Flow are:*
$$X_{k1t} = A_{kt} + \sum_{q} p_{q,k,1,1}\, X_{q,1,t-1} \qquad \text{(all k and t} >1) \quad (2)$$

The number of students at level 1 is equal to the number of admissions plus the number of internal transfers between programs.

Let T_{kst} = number of external transfers (including readmissions) into program k at level s during period t.

Then,

$$X_{kst} \sum_q p_{q,k,s-1,s} X_{q,s-1,t-1} + \sum_q p_{q,k,s,s} X_{q,s,t-1} + T_{kst}$$
$$\text{(all k, s, ang t} > 1) \quad (3)$$

This equation represents the flow of students at all other levels. In this form it does not accommodate digression in student level (from s to s − 1) or discontinuities in advancing to higher student levels (jumps from s to s + 2), but these can be included easily in additional terms. Basically, a term is necessary corresponding to each nonzero element of the transitional probability matrix, $\left\{ p_{q,k,s,n} \right\}$.

—*Initialization Contraints:*

$X_{ks1} = N_{ks1}$ = actual number of students in each field of study at level s at time $t = 1$. Since all X_{kst} for $t = 1$ are therefore constants, it is possible to reduce the dimensions of   (4) the formulation by substituting these values for X_{kst} throughout, although this will be somewhat unwieldy from an input parameter generation standpoint.

—*The constraints on degree production are:*

Let $d_{k,s}$ = probability of a degree being awarded to a student in field k at level s. (Assumes stationary probabilities.)

   D_{kt} = number of degrees in field k desired at time t (the specified degree production plan).

Then,

$$\sum_s d_{k,s} X_{kst} - y_{kt}^- + y_{kt}^+ = D_{kt} \qquad \text{(all k and t)} \quad (5)$$

Where, y_{kt}^- will be positive if the degree goal specified is exceeded, and y_{kt}^+ will be positive if the reverse is true.

—*The Objective Function:*

The goal is to come as close as possible to producing the number of degrees specified over the planning horizon, D_{kt}. Therefore, we use as an objective function:

$$\min Z = \sum_k \sum_t \; (y_{kt}^- + y_{kt}^+) \quad (6)$$

Either or both of y_{kt}^- or y_{kt}^+ will equal zero for a given k and t in the optimal solution.

Equations (1) through (6) above are expressed in a Linear Programming format and solution algorithms are readily available. While these are optimization techniques, it should be apparent that we are not optimizing a true institutional objective function.

The above formulation is of substantial size in terms of computational requirements. Assuming a 10-year degree plan is to be investigated at a level of disaggregation corresponding to the Program Category level specified in the NCHEMS Program Classification Structure (Gulko, 1970), we can approximate the dimensions on the indices as follows: $k = 30$, $s \cong 10$, $t = 20$, $i = 30$, $r = 10$, $j = 4$. Thus, the number of variables would be: $X_{kst} = 6000$, and $A_{kt} = 1{,}200$, or a total of 7,800.

The number of constraint equations on resources available would be approximately 6,000. It is possible to reduce the number of these equations by rewriting (1) as:

$$\sum_i \sum_j \sum_s \sum_k C_{ijr} \; a_{ijks} \; X_{kst} \le \mu_{tr}$$

This assumes that the resource distribution to the discipline areas is not made in advance. The distribution is, of course, available once the X_{kst}'s are determined. If this reformulation can be accomplished, the number of these equations is reduced to approximately 200. The modification does imply freedom to shift resources between different discipline areas if this would aid in attaining the degree output objective. Yet this may not, in fact, be feasible on a short-term basis. There are approximately 6,000 flow of student constraints (2, 3, and 4), and 600 degree output constraints (5), or a total of approximately 6,800 constraints assuming the above modification is made.

A version of the model for a hypothetical junior college has been developed and solved by David Henard (1971a), utilizing $k = 4$ fields of study; $s = 4$ levels of students; $t = 14$ time periods; $i = 7$ discipline programs; $r = 7$ resource types; and $j = 2$ course levels. The model formulation consisted of 392 structural variables and 395 constraint equations. It was run utilizing MPS/360–2 on an IBM 360/75 in 6.3 minutes, including tape-to-tape input/output times. The parametric programming capabilities of the model were successfully utilized during further investigations and are reported in a second paper (Henard, 1971b).

A very similar model could be used for short-range planning as well, since a decrease in t allows a corresponding increase in the level of disaggregation of fields of study. (For example, $t = 4$ and $k = 150$ is a model of approximately the same size as that presented above.)

The linear programming solution to this formulation will yield the admissions strategy (the A_{kt}'s) that will come as close as possible to attaining the specified degree production plan. The solution also yields the number of students at each level who will need to be maintained during all periods in each degree program, the X_{kst}'s. (This is not to imply, however, that the X_{kst}'s are control variables.) Likewise, the resource requirements for each period are obtained as part of the solution.

SOME GENERALIZATIONS

1. The formulation assumes that transfers from sources external to the institution being modeled (the T_{kst}'s) are specified constants. If they are

variables, the solution that optimizes the objective function will undoubtedly permit a disproportionately large number of transfers into the higher student levels, when resource constraints are binding.

It is possible to introduce some flexibility by allowing the T_{kst}'s to be variables while imposing stability constraints. For example, the following constraints would allow a 5 per cent deviation from each preceding year.

$$T_{kst} \leq 1.05\ T_{kst-1}$$
$$T_{kst} \geq .95\ T_{kst-1} \qquad \text{(all k, s, and t > 1)}$$
$$T_{ks1} = \text{Actual number of transfers during time period 1.}$$

2. Various parameters of the model are easily made time dependent if historical data can be obtained to support such a generalization. Specifically, the elements of the induced course load matrix could be redefined a_{ijkst} and incorporated in equation (1). Likewise, the transitional probabilities may be nonstationary, p_{qksnt} and equations (2) and (3) would be reformulated using these different values. Neither of these modifications increases the size of the model, but since parameter preparation for a linear programming run is a substantial task, and for this size problem would be accomplished on a computer, the effect of these modifications cannot be dismissed lightly.

3. Resources available to the discipline areas are considered to be time dependent and are thus written as μ_{itr}. It is recommended, however, that such variations be investigated parametrically as described below.

Resource conversions may vary over time, thus requiring the C_{ijr} to be expressed as time dependent, C_{ijrt}. While these are easily incorporated in the formulation, the time relationship probably cannot be readily determined; thus the assumption of stability of these ratios with time will likely be necessary.

4. The degree production constraints (5) can easily be expanded to include other degree types for graduate or professional students. This does increase the problem size considerably. It is felt that the various degree types can be modeled separately; the only difficulty is that of properly handling the resource constraints (1). Specifically, the institution's resources would have to be distributed to each degree type modeled.

PARAMETRIC PROGRAMMING

The most useful feature of the linear programming model is the ability to perform parametric investigations. Once the initial solution is obtained, many additional alternatives can simply be "read off" the final tableau or obtained with relatively few additional iterations. In addition, alternate optima and the associated allowable range on variables before a change in basis occurs are by-products of the final tableau. However, it is not so trivial to determine the ranges over which two or more variables may jointly vary before a basis change occurs. Specifically, parametric programming is suggested relative to the following elements:

1. *Available Resources.* One can easily study the effect on degree production as a result of making available additional resources (changing the

μ_{itr} vector) for those constraints (1) that have zero slack. In fact, the imputed values in the final tableau indicate an expansion path for adding resources within the context of the "pseudo" objective function. These elements also indicate those disciplines where an excess of resources has been made available in connection with a degree output plan. Further, those time periods, disciplines, and resource types that are "resource-rich," as indicated by corresponding nonzero slack variables, are immediately obvious.

2. *Transfer Students Specified.* Perhaps the best way to gain flexibility with regard to handling transfers, T_{kst} is through the study of feasible variations to a set of specified values. This involves parametric programming on the student flow constraint equations (3).

3. *Degree Production.* It is possible to vary the degree plan, represented by the D_{kt}'s, in a parametric fashion. This is perhaps the most useful investigation within the scope of the degree goal planning model. It allows one to study the resource and admissions decision implications of different degree production plans.

The objective function in equation (6) could be rewritten to include a different relative importance associated with the various degree production goals:

$$\min Z = \sum_k \sum_t \ W_k \ (y_{kt}^- + \ y_{kt}^+)$$

Where W_k = weight or importance associated with deviations from degree production plans in field of study k.

An even more flexible weighting scheme would be to express the objective function as:

$$\min Z = \sum_k \sum_t \ W_{kt}^- \ y_{kt}^- + \sum_k \sum_t \ W_{kt}^+ \ y_{kt}^+ ,$$

allowing degree deficits and surpluses in each time period to be weighted differently. Parametric programming on the objective function can then be utilized to investigate the effects of attaching levels of importance to deviations from certain types of degree output plans.

4. *Admissions.* While it is useful for a decision maker to have the ability to investigate the resource implications of degree outcome specifications, it is somewhat unrealistic to suppose that the solution values of the admissions variables (the A_{kt}'s) will automatically be satisfactory. That is, certain A_{kt}'s may appear in the final solution that could not be attained due to a limited student demand for admission into certain fields. Actually, the institutional planner must be concerned with an equilibrium between demands for educated students and demands for student admission. The model allows a flexibility to iteratively study this equilibrium problem in a number of ways. One could parametrically vary the A_{kt}'s resulting from an initial solution until they fell into an acceptable range, while at the same time noting the effect on the objective function. Or, one could express both goals in the same objective function by allowing deviations S_{kt}^+ and S_{kt}^- from a specified admission plan (A_{kt}'s expressed as constants) and rewriting equation (2) as:

$$X_{k1t} = A_{kt} + S_{kt}^+ - S_{kt}^- + \sum_q p_{q,k,1,1} X_{q,1,t-1}$$

The objective function would be reformulated as:

$$\min Z = \sum_k \sum_t \left[W_k (y_{kt}^- + y_{kt}^+) + W_k' (S_{kt}^- + S_{kt}^+) \right]$$

It is then possible to investigate parametrically the implications of different admissions specifications and degree specifications simultaneously.

THE RESOURCE MINIMIZATION MODEL

A related question, which is perhaps more important than minimizing deviations from degree production plans, is to minimize the resources required to obtain degree outputs that are "at least as great" as some acceptable level. The following modifications to the model formulated above will accomplish this purpose:

—Equation (1) remains the same with the exception that the μ_{itr} is now considered a variable rather than a specified parameter of the model.

—Equation (5) is rewritten as:

$$\sum_s d_{ks} X_{kst} \geq D_{kt} \qquad \text{(all k and t > 1)} \qquad (7)$$

and D should be interpreted as the "minimum acceptable level of degrees," as opposed to the "desired number of degrees."

—The objective function (6) is rewritten as:

$$\min Z = \sum_r \sum_t \sum_i \mu_{itr}$$

That is, the objective in this formulation is to minimize the total amount of all resources utilized over all time periods, which still yields an acceptable degree output plan. All other equations remain the same as expressed in the first model. Actually, the formulation of the resource minimization model would, in practice, be simplified by writing the objective function as:

$$\min Z = \sum_i \sum_t \sum_r \left[\sum_j \sum_s \sum_k C_{ijr} a_{ijks} X_{kst} \right] \qquad (8)$$

and eliminating the resource constraints (eqs. 1).

The generalizations presented above are also applicable to this model. Parametric programming on the D_{kt} vector is a particularly useful way to study an expansion path for degree production that will always minimize resources. It is judged that the resource minimization model and the degree goal planning model could be used interchangeably to evolve a long-range institutional plan.

A difficulty arises in the formulation of our objective function in (8) above as it relates to parametric investigation on the D_{kt} vector. Tradeoffs between resources are not accommodated. That is, the model simply minimizes the number of units of each resource type involved without consideration of the value of the resource. It should be noted that the model yields the "imputed value" of the resources, which is useful information for comparative purposes. However, one can change the objective function to:

$$\min Z = \sum_i \sum_t \sum_r m_r \; \mu_{itr}$$

where m_r = value (in dollars) per unit of resource type r. (This assumes the value does not change over time and is the same for all disciplines. This assumption is easily removed by simply defining m_{itr} = value per unit of resource r in discipline i at time t.)

THE OPTIMAL DISTRIBUTION OF RESOURCES TO DISCIPLINE DIVISIONS

Given that it is possible to determine the value per resource unit, m_r, then the degree planning model could be reformulated as follows:

—Rewrite inequality (1) as:

$$\sum_i \; \sum_j \; \sum_s \; \sum_k \; \sum_r m_r C_{ijr} \; a_{ijks} \; X_{kst} \le R_t \qquad \text{(all t > 1)} \qquad (9)$$

where R_t is the estimated total budget for all resources during time period t.

It is now reasonable to revert to the degree goal planning model and minimize deviations from desired degree outputs, which is the objective function specified in equation (6).

Once the X_{kst}'s are determined, the resource allocations to the departments can be directly calculated for each time period. Thus, the solution specifies how best to distribute a total estimated budget within the context of attaining a given degree production plan. Again, it is easy to study deviations in the R_t's by utilizing parametric programming.

STATEWIDE MODELS

Suppose the institutional models developed in the above sections are expanded by appending the subscript, c (to denote college or university), and the equations for all institutions are combined into one global formulation. For example:

X_{kstc} = number of students in degree program k at student level s during time period t in university or college c.

$a_{ijksc,}$ $C_{ijrc,}$ $A_{ktc,}$ P_{qksnc} and D_{ktc} are similarly redefined.

This expands the model substantially and probably renders it computationally infeasible if aggregation is not possible. The most reasonable dimension for aggregation would appear to be a combination of disciplines, i, and/or fields of study. k, into broader areas, although other aggregations of student levels or time periods would also need to be considered.

Putting aside the "size of the problem" difficulty, very few changes in addition to increasing the size of the formulation by the college/university subscript are needed to formulate the degree goal planning model for a state-wide system.

The degree production constraint must be modified to:

$$\sum_s \sum_c d_{ksc} X_{kstc} - y_{kt}^- + y_{kt}^+ = D_{kt} \quad \text{(all k and t} > 1) \quad (10)$$

where the desired degrees, D_{kt}, are specified for the entire state system rather than for the individual institutions. (Note the subscript c is not included.) The objective function remains:

$$\min Z = \sum_k \sum_t (y_{kt}^- + y_{kt}^+)$$

The model minimizes deviations from degree plan goals across the entire statewide system. The results of the model will specify how "best" to distribute degree production responsibilities across the system, keeping in mind, of course, that "best" is used in the context of an output deviation objective. The same types of parametric investigations discussed above are also applicable to the statewide model.

An enhancement to the statewide planning model would be to build into the formulation the ability to establish new programs at any of the institutions. Generally, a new program involves a nonrecurring "set-up" cost; that is, a fixed charge. This could easily be formulated as a mixed integer programming problem. Unfortunately, such a formulation is computationally infeasible for problems of the magnitude discussed in this paper. However, the idea may be more than just interesting from a theoretical standpoint, since certain alternative combinations of new programs can be run separately as linear programming problems.

SUMMARY AND CONCLUSIONS

The goal programming model allows a good deal of flexibility in testing the implications of various admission and degree output alternatives. It is intended to be used in an experimental mode; therefore, it finds utility in the same context as a cost simulation model. In this sense it has some of the same deficiencies. It is structurally quite similar. The induced course load matrix and the transitional probability matrix utilized in the formulation are subject to the same shortcomings; that is, the problems associated with obtaining historical data to construct these matrices, the questions of stability, etc., all remain.

In addition, the model has a conceptual defect in the linearity assumptions. In spite of the fact that the objective function is actually a pseudo expression of institutional objectives, one cannot escape the fact that a nonlinear formulation would be required to reflect reality.

As one considers the wide range of opportunities to investigate parametrically the different planning alternatives, he realizes that the linear programming approach is being utilized simply as an efficient search procedure, and optimality is a secondary issue. Thus, the utility of the model is highly dependent upon the development of procedures that allow variations to be investigated efficiently and easily after the initial solution is obtained. Carrying out the parametric studies in practice would be a confounding task unless an interface could be developed that would shield the decision maker from the traditional operations on the final tableau.

Since optimality is not a crucial issue, attention probably should be directed toward developing heuristic techniques that may improve the search efficiency and facilitate the parametric investigation. It also should be noted that heuristic approaches may allow the assumption of a linear objective function to be removed without imposing severe limitations on the solution procedure.

REFERENCES

Breneman, David and David Hopkins.
  1969   *The Stability of Faculty Input Coefficients in Linear Work Load Models of the University of California*, Ford Foundation Report No. 69–4 (Berkeley: University of California).
Gulko, Warren W.
  1970   *Program Classification Structure*, Preliminary Edition, NCHEMS Technical Report 13 (Boulder, Colorado: Western Interstate Commission for Higher Education).
Gulko, Warren W.
  1971   *The Resource Requirements Prediction Model 1 (RRPM-1): An Overview*, NCHEMS Technical Report 16 (Boulder, Colorado: Western Interstate Commission for Higher Education).
Henard, David E.
  1971A *The Solution of a Goal Programming Model for Junior College Planning* (Urbana, Ill.: University of Illinois Office of Space Programming).
Henard, David E.
  1971B *The Use of a Linear Programming Model for Simulating Future Budget Variations and Degree Output Increases* (Urbana, Ill.: University of Illinois Office of Space Programming).

ACADEMIC RESOURCE ALLOCATION MODELS AT UCLA*

by
James S. Dyer
University of California, Los Angeles

This paper provides a summary of efforts to develop academic resource allocation models by individuals at the Graduate School of Management (GSM) at UCLA. The primary focus of these efforts has been on the problem of allocating the activities of the faculty of an academic department among formal teaching at various course levels, departmental service duties (e.g., administration and curriculum development), and other tasks, such as research and administration. We found that the development of such a model was a straightforward task with one major exception: the objective function of the model involved multiple criteria. Thus, the development of a practical approach for dealing with multiple criteria in the context of a mathematical programming solution strategy became our most important secondary objective.

The academic departmental resource allocation model is described in the next section, along with a brief summary of the approach we have proposed for dealing with the multiple criteria that arise. This application suggested several topics for further research. Each of these topics is listed, and a brief summary of our efforts in dealing with each topic is presented in the following sections. Finally, we describe our current research activities in the area of educational administration.

THE DEPARTMENTAL MODEL

The departmental model is concerned with the allocation of faculty effort among various activities, given an exogenous budget for personnel in terms of Full Time Equivalent (FTE) positions. This allocation may be expressed in terms of course sections or "equivalent course sections," one unit of which is defined as the time and effort equal to the actual teaching of one course section. The use of nonacademic personnel or other resources, such as supplies and expenses, are not considered in this model.

* Support for this work was provided by a subgrant from the Ford Foundation Project for Research in University Administration, University of California at Berkeley. Major portions of the work summarized herein were performed by or under the leadership of A. M. Geoffrion. Other individuals who have contributed significantly to these efforts are J. P. Amor, A. Feinberg, W. W. Hogan, and J. Mulvey.

A Description of the Model

The model can be viewed as a linear programming problem with multiple objective functions. We assume that the allocation of academic FTE of each type (e.g., tenured regular faculty, nontenured regular faculty, teaching assistants, and lecturers) and the student enrollment in various programs (e.g., lower division, undergraduate, upper division undergraduate, masters, and Ph.D.) are determined exogenously to the model, perhaps by the campus administration. The departmental decision variables included in the model are the following:

1. The number of course sections offered at each level. The levels, for example, may correspond to lower division undergraduate, upper division undergraduate, first year masters program courses, second year masters program and elective courses, and Ph.D. seminars.

2. The number of regular FTE faculty of each type hired beyond the department's contractual commitments.

3. The number of irregular FTE faculty hired.

4. The number of equivalent FTE released from teaching for departmental service duties.

Some of the constraints in the model reflect obvious physical relationships. For example, the total number of course sections offered by the department is limited by the number of available FTE faculty. Further, the hiring of irregular faculty is limited by the available FTE generated by vacancies, leaves, and support from outside the department. Other constraints place a limit on the number of faculty hired, and provide that teaching releases of regular faculty cannot exceed the total teaching obligations.

Policies or commitments of the department are reflected by other constraints. We may require, for example, that a minimum number of sections must be offered at each course level. Similarly, we may place upper and lower bounds on the average class size at each level.

In the original version of our model, we included the number of course sections offered by the department at each level as individual criterion functions. More recently, we have replaced these values with average class sizes at the different course levels. In addition, we include as a criterion function the faculty effort devoted to major departmental service duties (here the equivalent course sections correspond to reduced teaching loads). Finally, the last criterion is the regular faculty effort devoted to activities such as research, student counseling, and minor administrative tasks, again measured in equivalent course sections. The mathematical details of this model are put forth by Geoffrion, Dyer, and Feinberg (1971–1972), and Feinberg (1972).

The Multi-Criterion Optimization Strategy

A general statement of the multiple criteria problem which we consider may be written

$$\max_{x \in X} U(f(x)) \tag{1}$$

where f is an r-dimensional vector of real valued criterion functions, x is an n-dimensional vector of real valued decision variables, X is the permissible region of R^n associated with x , and U is the decision maker's utility function defined on the range of f. We assume that U and each component of f are concave and continuously differentiable, that U is increasing in each f_i (perhaps requiring a change of sign), and that X is convex and compact.

Several "feasible directions" algorithms consist of a direction-finding subproblem and the choice of a "step-size" in that direction, the latter being a one-dimensional optimization problem. In a recent paper, Geoffrion (1971) notes that such an algorithm could be applied to (1) if the gradient of U with respect to f , $\Delta_f U(f(x^k))$, and an optimal solution to the stepsize problem were known at each iteration k (for details, see Geoffrion, Dyer, and Feinberg, 1971, 1972); a similar approach is proposed by Boyd (1970). A vector collinear with $\Delta_f U(f(x^k))$ can be determined if the decision maker answers the r − 1 questions, "With all other criteria held constant at the point $f^k = f(x^k)$, how much would you be willing to decrease the value of criterion i to obtain an increase of Δf_1^k in criterion 1?" The responses Δf_i^k , i = 2, . . . , r, allow the approximations

$$w_i^k = \frac{\partial U/\partial f_i \ \big|\, f = f(x^k)}{\partial U/\partial f_1 \ \big|\, f = f(x^k)} \cong \frac{\Delta f_1^k}{\Delta f_i}, \quad i = 1, \ldots, r,$$

to be made. The direction of the gradient of the objective function is generally sufficient for use in the direction finding subproblem of a feasible directions algorithm.

The decision maker must provide the solution to the one-dimensional stepsize problem. The values of the criteria over the closed interval may be presented graphically or at selected points along the grid. If the dimension of f is not great, the decision maker should be able to identify his preferred solution to this problem. This would complete one iteration, and the procedure could be updated until an optimum (or near optimum) solution is obtained.

The particular "feasible directions" algorithm selected for the implementation of this procedure is one proposed by Frank and Wolfe (1956). This algorithm may be applied to the problem max g(x) subject to the usual assumptions on g and z. At x∈Z
each iteration k , the subproblem

$$\max_{z \in Z} \Delta_x g(x^k)^T \cdot z \tag{2}$$

is solved for z^k, and $d^{k\Delta} = z^k - x^k$. A step-size $t^k \in \{0, 1\}$ is determined which maximizes $g(x^k + td^k)$; then, $x^{k+1} = x^k + t^k d^k$ and another iteration is performed. One obviously desirable feature of this algorithm is its computational simplicity. If Z is defined by a series of linear constraints (as in the case of the departmental model), (2) is a linear programming problem.

Experiences with the Model

A departmental model was developed on the basis of actual data from the 1970–71 operations of GSM at UCLA. An administrator provided the information required by the interactive solution strategy, and eventually determined his "most desirable" allocation of faculty resources for the 1971–72 academic year. Subsequently, the model was used to explore the implications of proposed reductions in departmental FTE, of certain significant changes in the design of the MBA program, and of the impact of introducing a part-time MBA program. The details of these studies are described by Feinberg (1972), while a single example of the use of the model is given by Geoffrion, Dyer, and Feinberg (1971–1972).

A similar departmental operating model was developed for the Department of Education at UCLA during the 1971–72 academic year. The reason for this second implementation was to explore the generality of the structural details of the model, and to gain experience in interacting with decision makers who were not familiar with either mathematical programming or utility theory. Again, the development of the model was a straight forward task, and the final result differed from the GSM model in only a few minor details. Further, after a brief "training" session, two administrators from Education experienced no difficulty in providing the information required by the interactive optimization procedure. The solution determined by these administrators differed significantly from the current operations of the Department, and it was presented to a committee for further study.

Extensions and Further Research

Our experiences with the departmental operating model suggested several topics for further study, including the following:

1. How can the interactive approach be used to coordinate resource allocation decisions in hierarchical or multi-level organizations?

2. What are the best experimental procedures for estimating tradeoffs between criteria?

3. What are the implications for the interactive solution strategy if decision makers are occasionally inconsistent or make slight "errors" in specifying the tradeoffs?

4. Since only a few iterations of the interactive procedure can be expected in practice, what are the *initial* rates of convergence for various mathematical programming algorithms with potential for interactive optimization?

5. What is the relationship between this interactive procedure and the goal programming approach for dealing with multi-criterion problems in higher education?
6. What is the relationship between this aggregate planning model and the more detailed problem of assigning faculty to specific courses?

We shall now summarize our efforts to deal with each of these questions in turn.

Interactive Optimization in Hierarchical Organizations

The use of the interactive optimization strategy for the coordination of two-level organizations with multiple objectives was first suggested by Geoffrion (1970) in the context of the academic resource allocation problem and later generalized by Geoffrion and Hogan (1972). In symbols, the overall university administration-academic departmental resource allocation problem can be written as

$$\max_{y \in Y} P\{ v^1 (y), \ldots, v^N (y) \},$$

where

$$v^\ell (y) \equiv \max_{x^\ell \in X^\ell (y)} U^\ell \left[f^\ell (x^\ell, y), \ldots, f^\ell_r (x^\ell, y) \right]$$

and

y = vector of allocation and perhaps other decision variables under the control of the administration (e.g., number FTE faculty to be allocated to each department, student enrollment ceilings for each department)

Y = the set of allowable choices for y (e.g., limits on total faculty FTE and student enrollment) and by administration policies (e.g., honor prior commitments to individual departments)

p = the administration's preference or utility function for choosing among alternative tradeoffs between the "values" v of decison vector Y to department ℓ

N = number of academic department ($\ell = 1 \ldots N$)

and x^ℓ, $X^\ell(y)$, f^ℓ_i, and U^ℓ have the same interpretations as in (1) and in the explanation of the departmental model.

The solution strategy suggested by Geoffrion and Hogan (1972) for this problem is based on interactive optimization, and can be viewed as a structured dialogue between the administration and the departments. Loosely speaking, a typical round of the dialogue consists of the administration asking the departments what would happen if Y were set at $\bar{y}$, to which the departments respond by giving some local information about the optimal solution of the corresponding departmental operating problem. The administration then uses this information in a prescribed manner to determine a revised trial value for y.

Experimental Procedures for Estimating Tradeoffs

The estimation of a "tradeoff" (or marginal rate of substitution) requires the decison maker to indicate how much he would "give up" from one criterion value in order to gain a specified increment in another. Torgerson (1958:52–58) argues that ordinal comparisons (e.g., I prefer A to B) are much less demanding on the decision maker than point estimates (e.g., I will give up 2 units of criterion 1 for 3 units of criterion 2). In addition, Feinberg (1972) has performed several experiments comparing alternative means of posing the tradeoff question to subjects. He found that the tradeoffs obtained from a series of ordinal comparisons were more accurate than those obtained from point estimates.

This strategy of using a series of ordinal comparisons to estimate tradeoffs was adopted by Dyer (1972, 1973) in the development of a time-sharing computer program written to implement the interactive approach to the solution of the multiple criterion problem. The tradeoff estimation routine in the time-sharing program creates a dialog between man and machine. The decision maker's responses to questions posed by the program reveal his tradeoffs without requiring that he be aware of their meaning or significance. Thus, the need for "training" the decision maker and the need for assistance by "experts" in the use of the interactive procedure are sharply reduced by the time-sharing program.

Due to arbitrary computer storage limitations on the time-sharing system at UCLA, the departmental model has not yet been implemented in the time-sharing mode. However, experiments with subjects attempting to solve a hypothetical problem involving multiple criteria suggest that untrained individuals do not find the program difficult to use. A brief description of the computer program is presented in Dyer (1973), while further details and a summary of experiences in using the program are given in a second paper by Dyer (1972).

The Effects of Errors in the Estimation of Tradeoffs

Implicit in the original development of the interactive strategy was the assumption that the decision maker could provide the tradeoff and stepsize information without error. This assumption is equivalent to the requirement that expressions of preference and indifference be transitive. Experiments have confirmed that decison makers seldom exhibit such consistency in their responses (e.g., see Feinberg, 1972).

In order to investigate the effects of response errors on the interactive approach, Hogan (1971) specified the conditions under which the Frank-Wolfe algorithm will converge to an optimal solution, given that the gradient of the objective function is not known exactly. Loosely speaking, his primary result shows that the error in the estimate must vanish in the limit in order to guarantee infinite convergence.

Dyer (1973) has extended Hogan's results by considering the case in which the error does not necessarily vanish. His results provide conditions under which the Frank-Wolfe algorithm will yield a sequence of points converging to the optimal solution, or terminate at or converge to a result whose potential error can be bounded even in the face of inconsistent responses. Thus, responses which reflect the "human element" in the form of random errors and inconsistencies do not appear to be a significant hinderance to the use of interactive optimization.

Initial Rate of Convergence

The results of Canon and Cullum (1968) regarding the assymtotic rate of convergence of the Frank-Wolfe algorithm are well known and indicate that this assymtotic rate may be quite slow. Of course, it is not the infinite convergence of the procedure that really matters in practical applications, since only a modest number of interactive iterations can actually be carried out. Rather, it is the *initial rate* of convergence which is of interest. Very little in known about the initial rate of convergence on mathematical programming algorithms in general, but for the Frank-Wolfe method the following intriguing result has been demonstrated by Wolfe (1970): if the objective function of (1) is boundedly concave (i.e., is concave and has continuous second derivatives on X and there is a uniform lower bound on all eigenvalues of the Hessian) and X is a bounded convex polytype, then for the first K iterations (k is unknown)

$$\left(\frac{V - U\{ f_1(x^k), \ldots, f_r(x^k)\}}{V - U\{ f_1(x^1), \ldots, f_r(x^1)\}} \right) \left(\le \right) \frac{1}{2^{k-1}}, \ k \le K,$$

where V is the optimal value of (1). This result has recently been extended for the case of a single iteration by Amor (1971). Taken together, these results on the assymtotic and initial rates of convergence have the intuitively appealing interpretation that if the objective function value is very far from the optimal solution, the difference will be sharply reduced at each iteration (at worst, it will be halved); however, as we approach the solution, the percentage reduction in this difference becomes much smaller. Finally, Dyer (1973) has shown that if unbiased errors occur in the estimate of the gradient, then the *mean* initial rate of convergence of the algorithm is equal to the initial rate of convergence determined by ignoring any error terms.

Interactive Optimization and Goal Programming

An alternative approach to dealing with multiple criteria is goal programming, which has been suggested for use in academic resource allocation problems by several authors, most recently by Lee and Clayton (1972). Dyer (1972) has noted that the assumptions required by a goal programming problem formulation are so restrictive that an optimal solution to (1) can be expected only in certain special cases. He then provides an extension of goal programming in the form of an algorithm which requires interaction with the decision maker. This algorithm is intended to provide a conceptual and theoretical link betwen goal programming and the interactive optimization strategy suggested by Geoffrion.

THE FACULTY-COURSE ASSIGNMENT PROBLEM

Our current research efforts are focused primarily on the problem of determining a detailed annual teaching schedule by assigning individual faculty to specific courses during specific quarters. This is a substantial problem in its own right, but the value of a solution strategy for it and the value of the departmental model are both enhanced by their complementarity.

Once the departmental model has been used to determine the aggregate allocation of faculty effort, a detailed schedule that implements this plan must be found. Further, it seems likely that by studying the detailed plan implied by a particular solution to the departmental model, the administrator may have further insights that would perhaps encourage him to modify certain tradeoffs, or to alter specific constraints in the aggregate model, and then "re-optimize." Thus, we foresee an interactive procedure which would have this form:

1. The administrator uses the departmental model to determine a trial allocation of faculty effort among the various activities.

2. Information from the solution to the departmental model provides constraints on the detailed teaching schedule, which is then determined. If no feasible solution to the detailed scheduling problem exists, or if the administrator expresses concern with some aspects of the solution, certain modifications may be made in the departmental model, and we return to step 1.

Thus, we are encouraged to provide an efficient means of generating these detailed annual teaching schedules.

The first attempt at providing a scheduling model for GSM was based on an integer programming formulation (see Mulvey, 1972). Although this approach might be practical for a smaller department, the integer programming model for GSM (with over 80 FTE faculty) has over one thousand variables. Thus, certain modifications in the model and the solution strategy would be required before even the most efficient integer programming code could be applied.

Mulvey (1973) has recently noted that the integer programming model he proposed has the structure of a network flow model with a few integer side constraints. If these troublesome side constraints were eliminated, algorithmic procedures exist (e.g., the out-of-kilter method) which could be used to solve the network flow problem efficiently even though it still involves over one thousand variables (arcs). The integer side constraints include such restrictions as the following:

1. The second course in a two course sequence should be offered only if the first course is offered.

2. Although a faculty member may be able to teach any of five different courses at the undergraduate level, he may not wish to teach more than two at that level during a particular academic year.

However, as Mulvey suggests, the network model can be run ignoring such restrictions. If, in an analysis of the output, the administrator notices one or more violations of such constraints, the network structure can be modified (merely by adding or deleting certain arcs) to impose the restrictions, and the problem can be re-optimized (a task which is very efficient in terms of computer time). Such a system would be particularly valuable if it were implemented in a time-sharing mode with input-output formats designed for use by non-technical personnel. This is our ultimate goal.

Figure 1 presents a diagram of the network model. There is one node for each faculty member, and three arcs from each of these nodes into nodes representing each quarter. The upper and lower limits on each arc are expressed in equivalent course sections. Thus, a 5, 5 restriction on an arc into a node corresponding to a particular faculty member indicates that he will teach exactly five courses during the academic year, and a 0, 2 restriction on the flow into a particular quarter indicates that he is willing to teach as many as two courses that quarter, or as few as zero.

Figure 1
COLLEGES OF APPLIED ARTS AND TECHNOLOGY

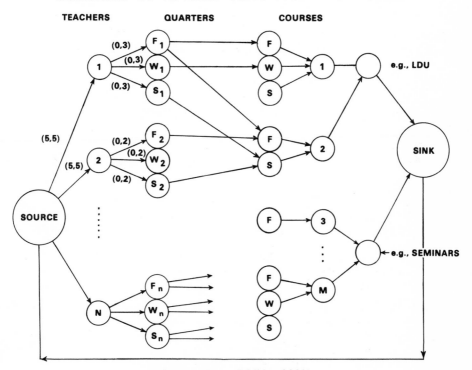

TOTAL MIN., TOTAL MAX.

There is also one node for each course offered by the department, and three nodes corresponding to the quarters preceding each of these. The existence of an arc from the "quarter node" of a particular faculty member to the corresponding "quarter node" of a particular course indicates that the individual can teach that course during that particular quarter. Further, upper and lower bounds on the flow of that arc, such as 0, 1, indicate the minimum and maximum number of sections of the course that he can be assigned to teach during that quarter. We can also place upper and lower bounds on the number of sections of each course that are offered during each quarter, and on the total number of sections of that course offered during the year.

Finally, there are arcs into nodes representing higher levels of aggregation corresponding to those used in the departmental model (e.g., lower division undergraduate courses (LDU), etc.). This provides the link between the departmental model and the detailed scheduling model. The result from the aggregate model may be used to determine the bounds on the flows from these nodes (e.g., we want 32 sections of lower division undergraduate courses). This important link is the basis for the iterative procedure that should lead to the final, simultaneous solution of both the aggregate resource allocation and the detailed faculty-course scheduling problems.

SUMMARY AND CONCLUSIONS

The inital efforts with the departmental resource allocation model raised certain questions and provided the basis for further research. Our current work with the faculty-course scheduling model suggests that the linkage of the two models should significantly enhance the value of both. After these models become operational in a form convenient for non-technical users, we may be in a position to address the two-level resource allocation problem as suggested by Geoffrion and Hogan (1972).

REFERENCES

Amor, J. P.
  1971   "On the Initial Rate of Convergence of Large-Step Methods of Feasible Directions," Discussion Paper No. 17, Operations Research Study Center, Graduate School of Management, University of California, Los Angeles.

Boyd, D.
  1970   "A Methodology for Analyzing Decision Problems Involving Complex Preference Assignments," Decision Analysis Group, Stanford Research Institute, Menlo Park, California.

Cannon, M. D., and C. D. Cullum.
  1968   "A Tight Upper Bound on the Rate of Convergence of the Frank-Wolfe Algorithm," *SIAM J. CONTROL*, Vol. 6, No. 4.

Dyer, J. S.
          "A Time-Sharing Computer Program for the Solution of the Multiple Criteria Problems." to appear in *Management Science*.

Dyer, J. S.
  1972   "An Empirical Investigation of a Man-Machine Interactive Approach to the Solution of the Multiple Criteria Problem," presented at the Seminar on Multiple Criteria Decision Making, South Carolina (proceedings to be published by the University of South Carolina Press).

Dyer, J. S.
  1972   "Interactive Goal Programming," *Management Science*, Vol. 19, No. 1.

Dyer, J. S.
1973   "The Effects of Errors in the Estimation of the Gradient on the Frank-Wolfe
        Algorithm, with Implications for Interactive Programming," Working Paper
        No. 196, Western Management Science Institute, University of California,
        Los Angeles.
Feinberg, A.
1972   "An Experimental Investigation of an Interactive Approach for Multi-
        Criterion Optimization with an Application to Academic Resource
        Allocation," Western Management Science Institute, University of California,
        Los Angeles.
Frank, M., and P. Wolfe.
1956   "An Algorithm for Quadratic Programming," *Naval Research Logistics
        Quarterly*, Vol. 3.
Geoffrion, A. M.
1970   "An Analytical Framework for Resource Allocation on a University Campus,"
        Discussion Paper, Graduate School of Management, University of California,
        Los Angeles.
Geoffrion, A. M.
1971   "Vector Maximal Decomposition Programming," Working Paper No. 164,
        Western Management Science Institute, University of California, Los
        Angeles.
Geoffrion, A. M., J. S. Dyer, and A. Feinberg.
1972   "An Interactive Approach for Multi-Criterion Optimization, with an
        Application to the Operation of an Academic Department," *Management
        Science*, Vol. 19, No. 4 (December 1972).
Geoffrion, A. M., J. S. Dyer, and A. Feinberg.
1971   "Academic Departmental Management: An Application of an Interactive
        Multi-Criterion Optimization Approach," Report P-25, Ford Foundation
        Program for Research in University Administration, Berkeley, California.
Geoffrion, A. M., and W. W. Hogan.
1972   "Coordination of Two-Level Organizations with Multiple Objectives,"
        in A. V. Balakrishnan (ed.), *Proceedings of the Fourth IFIP Colloquium on
        Optimization Techniques*, Academic Press.
Hogan, W. M.
1971   "Convergence Results for Some Extensions of the Frank-Wolfe Method,"
        Working Paper No. 169, Western Management Science Institute, University
        of California, Los Angeles.
Lee, S. M., and E. R. Clayton.
1972   "A Goal Programming Model for Academic Resource Allocation," *Manage-
        ment Science*, Vol. 18, No. 8.
Mulvey, J.
1973   Personal Communications.
Mulvey, J.
1972   "Preliminary Application of A Resource Allocation Procedure for the
        Educational Sector," Discussion Paper No. 21, Operations Research
        Study Center, Graduate School of Management, University of California,
        Los Angeles.
Torgerson, W. S.
1958   *Theory and Methods of Scaling*, John Wiley and Sons, New York.
Wolfe, P.
1970   "Convergence Theory in Nonlinear Programming," in J. Abagie, *Integer
        and Nonlinear Programming*, American Elsevier Puplishing Co., New York.

GOAL PROGRAMMING FOR ADMINISTRATIVE DECISIONS IN HIGHER EDUCATION

Sang M. Lee and Laurence J. Moore
Virginia Polytechnical Institute and State University

ADMINISTRATIVE DECISIONS IN HIGHER EDUCATION—THE SETTING

Institutions of higher learning in the United States have encountered more shocks and problems in recent years than perhaps any other segment of our society. The rapid expansion of colleges and universities, in terms of both size and quality, has had a profound impact on our entire society. In fact, never in the history of our country has society directed as much attention toward the broad area of higher education. Higher education is, today, a $10 billion a year enterprise which includes over eight million students, faculty, and staff (Abbey and Jones, 1969:67).

A number of forces, including professional and social pressures for a college-level degree, the desires and needs of our technical society, and the continuing thrust of modern research, have intensified the total demand for higher education in America. The financial needs and political power associated with higher educational institutions have caused all segments of the American public to observe the actions of these organizations with renewed and increasing interest.

The number of individuals enrolled in institutions of higher learning rose steadily during the decade of the 1960's. A recent study indicated that in the 1969–70 academic year there were over 7,750,000 students enrolled in the nation's 2500 colleges and universities (Parker, 1970:41–58). This figure represents approximately a five per cent increase over the total enrollment for the previous academic year. Whether this increase in enrollment can be expected to continue into the future has more recently been questioned, since the demand for college graduates has slackened in the early 1970's, and since young persons' attitudes toward higher education have shifted rather dramatically.

In any event, the higher education process continues to demand a greater proportion of the country's financial resources. This cost is being borne by students, taxpayers, and benefactors of the colleges and universities. A recent study reported that the average public institution of higher education budgeted operating funds totalling $14.6 million for the 1970 fiscal year (an increase from $12.7 million for the 1969 fiscal year), while its private counterpart budgeted an average of $5.5 million for the same period (up from $4.1 million for the 1969 fiscal year) (Binning, 1969:47–62). An increasing

121

number of institutions are being forced to raise tuition, intensify their search for financial donors, and seek additional tax-generated funds in order to finance the growing cost of higher education.

Contrary to the early 1960's, when there was generous support of higher education from many state legislatures, the federal government, and the public in general, the period from the late 1960's has been characterized by severe financial stringency for many institutions. In many cases, capital expansion budgets have been cut-off and operating budgets trimmed. There may be many reasons for this trend, such as the gradual reduction of federal research grants, and a faster rate of expenditure in higher education than the rate of increase in state revenues. Another important reason seems to be a switch of high priorities from higher education to more pressing social problems which require immediate attention of government. In addition, an over-supply of people with advanced degrees, such as Ph.D.'s, entering the academic job market in many areas of specialization, combined with a high proportion of tenured faculty in many departments, has resulted in drastically changing operational policies.

The final result of these events has been an increased awareness of, and interest in, the day-to-day operation of American institutions of higher education. One needs only to read a morning newspaper or watch an evening television news program to see that national, state, and local government officials, taxpayers, parents, and alumni are becoming increasingly anxious and concerned with the events occurring on our nation's campuses. Much of this attention centers on the administrative policies and procedures.

The crucial issues in the administration of higher education do not end at operational efficiency. Rather, they embody the very purpose, function, and concept of each educational institution (Crandall, 1969:112–120; Durstine, 1970; Weathersby and Weinstein, 1970). In essence, administrative policies are based on the combined philosophy of many conflicting interest groups providing inputs into the university, such as taxpayers, donors, administrators, faculty, students, staff, and users of university services.

DECISION ANALYSIS IN ACADEMIC INSTITUTIONS

The present situation in many universities is one of compromise and tense coexistence among all parties involved (Weathersby and Weinstein, 1970). Any effective decision model must, therefore, be capable of reflecting the various goals and priorities of the many interest groups seeking satisfaction.

The academic administrator must be able to demonstrate, to the various forces demanding justification for his actions, the basis for his decision process. This requires the development of a methodology which includes explicit consideration for the various multidimensional and often conflicting goals of the various interest groups. If the demands of the various forces are not met, the decision making methodology should illustrate why.

Any effective model must be capable of reflecting the priorities assigned to the desired goals within the constraints of the existing situation. The goal programming approach appears to be the most appropriate technique for developing a model to consider multiple, competitive, and often conflicting goals of varying priorities.

THE GOAL PROGRAMMING APPROACH

Goal programming (GP) is a special extension of linear programming (Charnes and Cooper, 1961; Ijiri, 1965; Lee, 1972). This method is capable of handling decision problems which deal with a single goal with multiple subgoals, as well as problems with multiple goals with multiple subgoals (Ijiri, 1965). In the conventional linear programming method, the objective function is undimensional—either to maximize profits (effectiveness) or to minimize costs (sacrifice). The GP model handles multiple goals in multiple dimensions; therefore, there is no dimensional limitation of the objective function.

Often, goals set by the decision maker are achievable only at the expense of other goals. Furthermore, these goals are incommensurable. Thus, there is a need to establish a hierarchy of importance among these incompatible goals so that the lower order goals are considered only after the higher order goals are satisfied or have reached the point beyond which no further improvements are desirable. If the decision maker can provide an ordinal ranking of goals in terms of their contributions or importance to the organization, the problem can be solved by GP.

In GP, instead of trying to maximize or minimize the objective criterion directly, the deviations between goals and what can be achieved within the given set of constraints are to be minimized. In the simplex algorithm of LP, such deviations are called "slack" variables. These deviational variables take on a new significance in GP. The deviational variable is represented in two dimensions, both positive and negative deviations from each subgoal or goal. Then, the objective function becomes the minimization of these deviations, based on the relative importance or preemptive priority weights assigned to them. However, the objective function may also include real variables with ordinary or preemptive weights in addition to the deviational variables.

The primary characteristic of GP is that it allows for an ordinal solution. Stated differently, management may be unable to obtain information on the cost or value of a goal or a subgoal, but often upper or lower limits may be stated for each subgoal. Usually the manager has judgment to determine the priority of the desired attainment of each goal or subgoal and rank them in ordinal sequence. Economically speaking, the manager works with the problem of the allocation of scarce resources. Obviously, it is not always possible to achieve every goal to the extent desired by management. Thus, with or without GP, the manager attaches a certain priority to the achievement of a certain goal. The true value of GP is, therefore, the solution of problems involving multiple, conflicting goals according to the manager's priority structure.

The general GP model can be mathematically expressed as (see Ijiri, 1965):

$$\text{Minimize } Z = \sum_{i=1}^{m} \left(d_i^+ + d_i^- \right)$$

subject to $Ax = Id^+ + Id^- = b, x, d^+, d^- \geq 0$,

where m goals are expressed by an m component column vector $b = (b_1, b_2, \ldots, b_m)$, A is an m × n matrix which expresses the relationship between goals and subgoals, x represents variables involved in the subgoals ($x_1, x_2, \ldots, x_n$), d^+ and d^- are m-component vectors for the variable representing deviations from goals, and I is an identity matrix in m dimensions.

The manager must analyze each one of the m goals considered in the model in terms of whether over- or under-achievement of the goal is satisfactory. If over-achievement is acceptaple, d_i^+ can be eliminated from the objective function. On the other hand, if under-achievement is satisfactory, d_i^- should not be included in the objective function. If the exact achievement of the goal is desired, both d_i^+ and d_i^- must be represented in the objective function.

The deviational variables d_i^+ and d_i^- must be ranked according to their preemptive priority weights, from the most important to the least important. In this way the lower order goals are considered only after the higher order goals are achieved as desired. If goals are classified in k ranks, the preemptive priority factor P_j (j = 1, 2, ..., k) should be assigned to the deviational variables, d_i^+ and d_i^-. The priority factors have the relationship of $P_j > > > P_{j+1}$ (= 1, 2, ..., k), which implies that the multiplication of n (however large it may be) cannot make P_{j+i} greater than or equal to P_j Of course, it is possible to refine goals even further by the means of decomposing the deviational variables. To do this, additional constraints and additional priority factors are required.

One more step in the procedure to be considered is the weighting of those deviational variables at the same priority level, i.e., variables with the same P_i coefficient. The criterion to be used here is the minimization of the opportunity cost or regret. This implies that the coefficient of regret σ, which is positive, must be assigned to the individual deviational variables on the same goal level. The coefficient σ_i simply represents the relative amount of unsatisfactory deviation from the goal.

APPLICATION OF GOAL PROGRAMMING TO ACADEMIC ADMINISTRATION

Two applications of goal programming to decision analysis in academic administration will be briefly discussed. The first relates to a general resource allocation planning model for an academic college (i.e., College of Business), which is presented in detail by Lee and Clayton (1972:B395–B408). The second application includes a modeling process for the university admissions decision process, and is given by Lee and Moore (1972).

A GOAL PROGRAMMING MODEL FOR ACADEMIC RESOURCE ALLOCATION

The purpose of the resource allocation GP model was to allocate the total payroll budget of an academic college among the various faculty, staff, and graduate assistants, while considering the numerous different goals of the college. The goals were identified as accreditation by the AACSB; adequate salary increases; desired faculty/student ratios; desired distribution of academic staff with respect to rank; desired faculty/staff ratio; desired faculty/graduate assistant ratio; and minimization of cost.

Constraints were specified which related the variables identified (i.e.) assistant professors; associate professors; full professors; graduate assistants; staff; etc.) to the various goals. The constraints included consideration for accreditation; total number of academic staff; distribution of academic staff; number of staff; number of graduate assistants; salary increase; and total payroll budget. The model formulation and results are given in Lee and Clayton (1972:B395–B408).

A GOAL PROGRAMMING MODEL FOR UNIVERSITY ADMISSIONS PLANNING

The purpose of the university admissions GP model was to arrive at a mix of students to be admitted into the university, while considering a multitude of economic and noneconomic goals reflecting the university's overall admission policies. The several goals identified for inclusion in the model were related to state residency requirements; university admission standards; residency hall occupancy rates; physical plant utilization; admission of female students; and transfer student admission.

The decision environment was described by the constructing of goal-constraints, including state residency; admissions standards; physical plant; student mix; residency hall capacity; and transfer-student mix. The variables of the model were defined to be applicants, broken down into categories according to sex; in-state *versus* out-of-state residency; freshmen *versus* transfer students; new applicants *versus* readmitted students; and multiple classifications of the above. The model formulation, solution results, and discussion are given in Lee and Moore (1972:390–395).

PROBLEM AREAS IN ACADEMIC ADMINISTRATION TO WHICH GOAL PROGRAMMING MIGHT BE PRODUCTIVELY APPLIED

The following is suggested as several types of problems in academic administration in which goal programming might be fruitfully applied. However, no attempt has been made to list exhaustively the areas for meaningful research.

(A) Resource allocation problem

Resource allocation problems exist at all levels of academic administration. The rising expenditure of higher education has caused lawmakers and the public to develop a keener and more critical view of the operation efficiency of educational institutions. Institutions can no longer request prodigious sums of money from the legislature without clear justification in terms of viable goals, alternatives, and expected results. One of the most important functions of the university administrator is to acquire the funds to cover ever increasing operational costs. The increasing financial pressure has greatly enhanced the importance of efficient resource allocation on the part of the institutions. Some resource allocation problem areas suggested are:

1. At the macro-level:

    (a) Among institutions,

    (b) Among categories of identified missions, such as: teaching, research, and extension activities.

2. At the micro-level:

    (a) Among university colleges,

    (b) Among college departments,

    (c) Among faculty positions within:

        (1) A university,

        (2) A college,

        (3) A department.

(B)   Blending or mix problems

It is, in many cases, impossible to distinguish between the type (A) problem and the type (B) problem. However, a problem may be predominantly of one type or the other, or a combination of the two. Some blending problems which may be addressed by the goal programming approach are:

1. Student-mix:

    (a) Admissions policies,

    (b) Student counselling with regard to academic major, course work, and occupational goals.

2. Faculty mix, with regard to:

    (a) Hiring policy and decisions,

    (b) Tenure policy and decisions,

    (c) Promotion policy and decisions.

3. Facility mix:

    (a) Physical plant,

    (b) Computer,

    (c) Library,

    (d) Research equipment.

(C)   Scheduling problems

Again, the scheduling problem will most probably be integrated into the resource allocation, blending problems. The decision analysis model for administrative decision making cannot be static; it must include consideration for the timing of the various resource inputs (physical and human) and the product outputs (students and research). Scheduling proplems which require the attention of administrators in higher education should include:

1. Scheduling of graduate output:

    (a) Undergraduate degrees,

    (b) Graduate degrees,

    (c) Engineering, Business, Liberal Arts, Education, etc.

2. Scheduling of nonstudent output:

    (a) Research,

    (b) Extension activities.

3. Scheduling of faculty inputs:

    (a) Senior faculty,

    (b) Junior faculty,

    (c) Instructors,

    (d) Graduate assistants.

4. Scheduling of nonfaculty inputs:

    (a) Buildings,

    (b) Equipment,

    (c) Books.

(D)   Transportation and logistics problems

One or more of the preceding problems may be viewed as a transportation or logistic type problem in that it deals with the supply of various types of services from various sources to various customers at various locations.

All of the above suggested areas of potential application for goal programming are, to some extent, sub-sets of one another. Different problems may be viewed productively as one of a certain type.

CONCLUSION

Virtually all models developed for university management have focused upon the analysis of input (resource) requirements. They have generally neglected or often ignored the system outputs, unique institutional values, and bureaucratic decision structures. However, these are important environmental factors which greatly influence the decision process. In this paper the GP approach is proposed because it allows the optimization of goal attainments while permitting an explicit consideration of the existing decision environment.

Developing and solving the GP model points out where some goals cannot be achieved under the desired policy and, hence, where tradeoff must occur due to limitations. Furthermore, the model allows the administrator to review critically the priority structure in view of the solution derived by the model. Indeed, the most important property of the GP model is its great flexibility which allows model iteration with numerous variations of constraints and priority structures of goals.

The GP approach is not the ultimate solution for all budgeting and planning problems in an academy. It requires that administrators be capable of defining, quantifying, and ordering objectives. The GP model simply provides the best solution under the given constraints and priority structure. Therefore, some research questions concerning the identification, definition, and ranking of goals still remain. There is the need for future research to develop a systematic methodology to generate such information.

The purpose of this paper is to demonstrate the application potential of GP to complex decision problems in university management. No doubt, each constraint requires an in depth analysis and it may well be a research area in itself. Furthermore, departmental interactions, boundary conditions, the administrator's own preferences, and the bureaucratic decision structure are important areas which require continuing research.

REFERENCES

Abbey, D., and E. R. Jones.
  1969   "On Modeling Educational Institutions." *The Bulletin of the Institute of Management Science*, 15:67.
Binning, Dennis W.
  1969   "1969–1970 College Operating Practice Analysis." *College and University Business*, 47:47–62.
Charnes, A., and W. W. Cooper.
  1961   *Management Models and Industrial Applications*, Vols. I, II. New York: Wiley.
Crandall, R. H.
  1969   "A Constrained Choice Model for Student Housing." *Management Science*, 16:112–120.
Durstine, R. M.
  1970   *Modeling the Allocation Process in Education*. Cambridge, Mass.: Center for Studies in Education and Development, Graduate School of Education, Harvard University.
Ijiri, Y.
  1965   *Management Goals and Accounting for Control*. North-Holland, Amsterdam.
Lee, Sang M.
  1972   *Goal Programming for Decision Analysis*. Philadelphia: Auerbach Publishers, Inc.
Lee, Sang M., and E. R. Clayton.
  1972   "A Goal Programming Model for Academic Resource Allocation." *Management Science*, 8:B395–B408.

Lee, Sang M., and L. J. Moore.
  1972   "A Model for Administrative Decision Making in Academic Institutions."
          *Proceedings of the Fourth Annual Meeting of the American Institute of
          Decision Sciences:390–395.* New Orleans: American Institute of Decision
          Sciences.
Parker, G. G.
  1970   "Statistics of Attendance in American Colleges and Universities,
          1969–1970." *School and Society,* 98:41–58.
Weathersby, G. B., and M. C. Weinstein.
  1970   *A Structural Comparison of Analytical Models for University Planning.*
          Ford Foundation Research Project in University Administration, Paper
          P-12. University of California.

THE APPLICATION OF MATHEMATICAL MODELS
TO ACADEMIC DECISION MAKING

James G. Morris and J. Randall Brown
Kent State University

INTRODUCTION

This paper attempts to summarize and synthesize the extensive discussions which took place at three free-flowing sessions on the relevance of mathematical modeling to academic decision making. These discussions occurred during the 1973 conference on "Decision Sciences in Academic Administration" held at Kent State University. Responsibility for errors of omission or misinterpretation rests, of course, with the authors.

THE NEED FOR SPECIFICITY IN GOAL DEFINITION

Program budgeting and cost simulation models developed for use in academic administration generally. link outputs to inputs in a deterministic sense. Planning is then accomplished using "what would happen if" approaches which focus on the sensitivity of the modeled system's output measures to input variations. In contrast, mathematical models, such as those described at the conference by Robert Wallhaus, Sang Lee, and James Dyer, are optimization models. They therefore seek ways to obtain desired output objectives as a function of inputs.

This latter approach requires the explicit definition of goals and objectives since a numerical measure must ultimately be used to determine the magnitude of deviations from their attainment. Also, a hierarchy of goals must be developed in order to define a measure of efficiency for the "solution" to the problem which has the proper sensitivity to the entirety of objectives. The question arose: Are administrators ready to accept and use this second point of view for modeling rather than the "what if" approach?

A participant reported that his initial research into implementing a mathematical modeling approach to academic resource allocation indicated that various college administrators within a large university had not specifically considered the questions of goal definition and preference orderings among them. Overtly it seemed that administrative effort was devoted to maintaining the status quo. There appeared to be no resistance to specific goal definition but this had not previously been done.

Such passivity will not suffice in the future as educational administrators are increasingly called upon to explain and justify the amount of public funding they request. Explicit goal definition is very important to growing institutions which require increasing levels of public support. However, it can also be argued that institutions in a steady state of growth have more difficulty attracting increased funding and must, therefore, allocate scarce resources even more efficiently over some particular mix of expenditure items. This requires very specific goal definition.

A methodology for facilitating the transitions to specific goal-oriented administration was suggested in a number of recent studies under the sponsorship of The Educational Testing Service.[1] The technique is based on a suggested inventory of goals and objectives to be considered—some such inventories have as many as 80 components. A form of the delphi method is then used which allows the president, other administrators, faculty members, members of the community, and students to interact in the determination of an overall ranking of these goals.

Such an inventory of goals usually includes overall goals for the institution, whereas there may exist unique departmentally-defined goals. There may also be departmentally determined ways to meet overall institutional goals. Thus, separation by organizational levels appears necessary in studies of goal definition, interpretation, and methods of achievement.

PROBLEMS OF IMPLEMENTING MATHEMATICAL MODELS

Goal programming can be quite useful as a mathematical modeling technique for goal-oriented administration. This approach to the allocation of scarce resources facilitates analyses aimed at determining how to come as "close as possible" to meeting conflicting goals which may be defined hierarchically. Additionally, maximally acceptable deviations from goal attainment can be treated as constraints using the goal programming approach. Initial academic users include colleges within Carnegie-Mellon University, The University of California at Los Angeles, and Virginia Polytechnical Institute and State University. Available evidence indicates mathematical models will not be used unless supported by university planning committees and/or top administrators. One reason for this is that most departments lack the technical capabilities to support the modeling effort, while one "expert" in the planning department may be sufficient to maintain the models for a university.

An important barrier to implementation is that the analyst's perception of problems does not match that of the person who is going to be using the model. There appears to be a mis-match between the decision maker's action-oriented perception of planning and decision making and the analyst's more systematic and analytical view of the process. Perhaps the implementation of planning models should be accomplished on a piece-wise basis (implement the first stage of the model before the second stage is attempted). This would seem especially reasonable in the case of a mathematical optimization approach which typically becomes infeasible for treating the

---

[1] Norman P. Uhl, "Identifying Institutional Goals: Encouraging Convergence of Opinion Through the Delphi Technique," *Research Monograph No. 2* Durham, North Carolina: National Laboratory for Higher Education, 1971.

totality of variables in a complex system. That is, mathematical approaches have typically found success when applied to the optimization of segments of systems.

FURTHER CONSIDERATIONS FOR APPLICATION OF MATHEMATICAL MODELING TECHNIQUES

Output Measures

The use of mathematical models implies a need for the development of useful output measures of a university in order to relate these measures to effectiveness and ultimately to controllable variables. One suggestion is to start using *some* output variables or proxies of them with which administrators feel comfortable without being overly concerned about validity or inherent cause and effect relationships. An example of this approach is the economists' use of the Dow Jones Industrial Average to measure economic activity. They use it for decision making in a macro sense even through they don't attribute complete validity to it. As outcome variables are used and analyzed in conjunction with cost, it is expected that more valid measures will evolve.

Costs

The computer cost per run of the RRPM and CAMPUS simulation models is much greater than for the goal programming and academic resources allocation models presented at the conference. Also, the collection of data and the modeling effort needed for RRPM and CAMPUS is very expensive and time consuming. A great distance lies between having the requisite data base and using these models for planning. Perhaps one benefit of a mathematical modeling approach is the development of simpler ways to use the available data to gain insights rather than having to use a large complex cost simulation model. A recent example is contained in an address given at the MAA (Mathematical Association of America) meetings in August, 1972 by John Kemeny—a mathematician and president of Dartmouth College. Working with the relatively simple concept of transition probabilities for moving from one academic rank to the next, he was able to show quite clearly the relationship between the proportion of the faculty which is tenured and the proportion of faculty members that are allowed to reach tenure from an initial appointment.

Data

The output from macroscopic simulation models such as RRPM may not presently be sufficiently detailed to provide input to more narrowly defined mathematical models, but this difficulty could be overcome. For example, scheduling systems could interact with RRPM if the level of output detail were adapted to the scheduling systems' needs. Apparently no funding or significant effort has been directed toward such interactions.

User Interaction

Finally, it is important to recognize that sometimes the performance of mathematical optimization models can be significanlty improved by allowing for interaction with the decision maker during the solution process. This interaction solution strategy is highlighted in James Dyer's paper.

It was noted that the faculty assignment aspect of Dyer's resource allocation model serves to tie together departmental decision making. There are really two decisions made at the departmental level and they are made at two points in time. One concerns what level of resources is to serve as the basis for negotiations "up the line." Then, when the resources become available, a decision must be made on how to assign them.

SUGGESTED AREAS FOR FURTHER RESEARCH

Objective Functions

One may question the appropriateness of the goal programming procedure for coming "as close as possible" to a set of conflicting goals by minimizing what amount to absolute deviations from goal attainment. A quadratic loss function (squares of deviations from goals) was suggested as a possible alternative objective function form. Efficient mathematical techniques are available to handle programming problems with quadratic objective functions subject to linear constraints. An area for future research is the comparison of the effect on decision making of objective function forms which imply different sensitivities to deviations from goals.

State Variables

Is the state of the student in the system defined in a useful way in present student flow models which use only the student's level and major? Perhaps additional state variables, such as financial aid levels, aspiration levels, and grade point levels, might provide valuable insights.

Student Flow Models

No one has done a study on the sensitivity of results in student flow models to changes in the probabilities of transition from one state to another. The induced course load matrix (ICLM) model associated with RRPM makes the same assumptions as Markov chain analysis. These assumptions (stable transition probabilities and one period dependence) may be inappropriate and the necessary data may not be available or have the required precision. More research is needed on methods of forecasting student flows. The forecasting techniques of ICLM depend heavily on historical data and cannot cope with unusual exogenous events. Thus, any forecasting schemes should allow for updating historical forecasts in light of current information.

Student flow models are designed to predict the effects of enrollment levels and mixes in one period on enrollment levels and mixes in some future period for use in "what if" approaches to planning. Perhaps it would be useful to develop models which reverse this mechanism and can be used to determine ways to *control* enrollment mixes. Thus certain curricula may have as a goal at least (or at most) a given number of graduates in a given period of time. Goal programming may be a way to do this. The current form of student flow models could enter the goal programming model as a subset of constraints. For example, the number of June, 19XX engineering graduates could be stated as a goal to be attained by adjusting the mix of students admitted to the university or to various programs at specified times. Using transition probabilities for student movements through the system, this goal could be treated as a constraint in an overall model.

Other Areas for Future Research

Other promising areas of research for mathematical models include:

a. facilities planning;

b. scheduling;

c. transportation systems;

d. unit costing of programs;

e. enrollment forecasting (all four components of enrollment forecasting, new students from high school, transfer students, dropout students who return, and the supply and demand for each degree program should be studied);

f. optimization studies of non-faculty cost components, such as inventory.

APPENDIX

Conferees at the Conference
PARTICIPANTS FROM OTHER UNIVERSITIES

Ageloff, Roy	University of Rhode Island
Alexander, Madelyn D.	University of Colorado
Antiocha, Sergio	Eastern Michigan University
Arnold, Walter	W. Arnold Associates
Bareither, Harlan	University of Illinois
Barnett, Robert	Systems Research Group
Bartes, James	Ohio State University
Baugman, Wayne E.	University of Pittsburgh
Christopher, David	University of Mississippi
Dold, Charles N.	University of Illinois
Dyer, James S.	University of California
Escarraz, Donald R.	University of Georgia
Foreman, Leslie	Systems Research Group
Gibbs, Thomas	Systems Research Group
Hardy, Stanley T.	Ohio State University
Heetderks, John A.	University of Wisconsin
Hubbard, Charles	Ohio University
Huckfeldt, Vaughn	NCHEMS—W.I.C.H.E.
Innus, Voldemar	State University of New York at Buffalo
Jewett, Frank I.	California State University
Jones, Clarence	Duquesne University
Jordon, Jack	University of Kentucky
Lee, Sang	Virginia Polytechnic Institute
Lord, Robert J.	Dartmouth College
MacGregor, Ian	University of Akron
McKinney, John	University of Cincinnati
Megley, John	Southern Illinois University
Moore, Laurence	Virginia Polytechnic State University
Naidu, G. M.	University of Wisconsin
Paranka, Stephen	Colorado State University
Rodgers, William	University of Wisconsin
Rogers, James L.	North Texas State University
Ross, Edwin	University of Pittsburgh
Schroeder, Roger	University of Minnesota
Scotton, Donald W.	Cleveland State University
Suslow, Sidney	University of California—Berkeley
Tabor, Dwight	Georgia State University
Thomas, Warren	State University of New York at Buffalo
Wallhaus, Robert	NCHEMS—W.I.C.H.E.

Photosetting by Thomson Press (India) Limited,
New Delhi.